313 Ways
to Slash Your
Business Overheads

313 Ways

to Slash Your Business Overheads

A bright idea for every
day of the year (with
one day off a week!)

GARY LONG

The McGraw·Hill Companies

Sydney New York San Francisco Auckland
Bangkok Bogotá Caracas Hong Kong
Kuala Lumpur Lisbon London Madrid
Mexico City Milan New Delhi San Juan
Seoul Singapore Taipei Toronto

Text © 2003 Gary Long
Illustrations and design © 2003 McGraw-Hill Australia Pty Ltd
Additional owners of copyright are acknowledged on the Acknowledgments page.

National Library of Australia Cataloguing-in-Publication data:

Long, Gary (Gary Allan John)
313 ways to slash your business overheads.

ISBN 0 074 71313 2.

1. Overhead costs. 2. Cost control.

I. Title.

658.1553

Published in Australia by
McGraw-Hill Australia Pty Ltd
Level 2, 82 Waterloo Road, North Ryde NSW 2113
Acquisitions Editor: Javier Dopico
Production Editor: Rosemary McDonald
Editor: Tess Hardman
Proofreader: Tim Learner
Internal design: Greg Gaul
Cover design: Jan Schmoeger/Designpoint
Typeset in Humanist 521 by Greg Gaul
Printed on 70 gsm bulky woodfree by Pantech Limited, Hong Kong.

The *McGraw-Hill* Companies

Contents

Preface

The sign on the shop window read 'For Lease—Prime Retail Space'.

Three weeks earlier this vacant shop lot had been alive with activity—its shelves were packed with the latest fashions, sales staff scurried to assist customers, and a stereo pumped out the latest hits, creating a fun and vibrant atmosphere. It was a bustling, successful business—or so I thought.

I contacted the realtor and inquired as to the fate of the occupant. 'Did they move to a better location?' I asked.

'No,' she responded in a matter-of-fact tone. 'Just another case of a business gone bust.'

This wasn't anything new to the realtor. In fact, it was a scenario she had witnessed time and time again. This story is all too familiar for most of us in business. We have all heard the horror stories and we may even have been part of one ourselves.

The statistics speak for themselves—the majority of small- to medium-sized businesses will not survive past their third year of operation. The reasons why businesses fail are many and varied; however, there is one common factor that exists in every case: the distinct lack of attention given to the cost of running a business.

How did this book come about?

Over the last eighteen years I have worked in the not-for-profit sector, in local and state government, in local and international private enterprise and as the owner of a small business. Working in such diverse industries has shown me that they all have one thing in common—the desire to keep operating costs to a minimum.

What is certain in today's competitive marketplace is that if your business or organisation is to survive, it must effectively manage its operating expenses. By lowering overheads you will create a competitive advantage for your business, enabling you to overcome the daily challenges of going head-to-head with your competition, maintaining profitability during a period of slow sales or establishing a new business. Surprisingly, there are very few resources available to assist the small business operator to keep their operating expenses in check.

Who should read this book?

If you are currently running a small business either as an owner or manager, or you are planning to start your own small business, then this is the book for you.

In writing this book I have kept the needs of the businessperson as the main objective. The 313 creative and low-cost ideas are proven winners that will help save you time and money and keep your sanity in check as you go about your daily business. Each practical idea is the result of years of personal experience and research.

Developing a cost-conscious culture

Controlling costs is not just a case of cutting expenses to save money. It's about developing a culture within your business that is committed to eliminating inefficiencies, minimising wastage, reducing loss and investing your money in purchases that will give you the maximum return on every dollar spent.

Developing a cost-conscious culture within your business takes time and patience. There are four common elements that all cost-conscious businesses need to have in order to continually minimise expenses and maximise productivity.

Communication

Talk, listen, listen, talk. Communication is the core factor to the success of most endeavours and developing a cost-conscious culture for your business is no different. You need to explain the reasons why specific cost-cutting strategies are being introduced. If your employees, suppliers and customers understand the justification behind your actions, they are more likely to support them. It is essential that employees believe they are being given the *full story* and feel free to ask questions or seek clarification on any issue. Employees and management should be updated regularly on the progress of your cost-saving activities.

By promoting free and active communication, you will empower your employees to put forward ideas of their own, participate in working groups and assist in the implementation of specific strategies.

Commitment

The success of your cost-cutting program necessitates a commitment from everyone connected with your business. You, your employees, your suppliers, your business partners and even your customers can all play a vital role in keeping expenses in check.

One of the main challenges with most cost-saving processes is that once they get started there is often not enough energy within the business to keep them going through to completion. To guarantee the successful completion of your cost-saving initiatives, you must put in place personnel whose goal it is to champion the cause. As the proprietor of your own small business, this responsibility would most likely be yours. In larger organisations it would usually fall to several individuals or a specially designated group.

Clear goals and a corresponding time frame should be established to effectively measure the success of cost-saving strategies.

Consistency

It's one thing to implement a few cost-saving ideas here and there. It's another to have a system in place that ensures your business will save money at every possible opportunity and do so over an extended period of time. Don't be 'penny wise and pound foolish' as there's no point in achieving savings in one area of your business if you are blatantly wasting money or resources in another. Your business should also continue to reduce expenses regardless of whether times are good or bad.

Celebration

Enjoy the results of cost-saving efforts and celebrate your successes. Reward your employees for any great ideas they put forward that result in considerable savings for your business. Promote a profit-sharing scheme among your employees if cost-saving goals are met. Highlight employees who contribute suggestions by awarding certificates or placing their photos in your staff newsletter or on the noticeboard. At the very least, a simple 'well done' and 'thank you' go a very long way.

How to get the most from this book

If you are holding this book in your hands, you have taken the first step on the road to a more profitable and cost-conscious business. However, if you are like many of the business owners I know, time is one of your most valuable commodities. The book has been written with this is mind. The 15 chapters each cover a separate area of cost saving, allowing you to locate specific strategies quickly and easily. You can read the book from cover to cover, hop from one chapter to another or implement an idea a day. As you read this book you should be constantly asking yourself, 'How can I best implement this strategy in my business?' Jot down these ideas next to each strategy or write them in your journal so you can refer to them later. You can implement them as they are presented or adapt them to suit your specific needs.

You have all the information you need to cut costs right here in your hands so there is no need to reinvent the wheel. It's now just a matter of putting these valuable ideas into practice within your business and making them work for you.

Acknowledgments

Firstly, I would like to express my sincere thanks to those individuals who offered their ideas, thoughts, successes and failures for the betterment of businesses everywhere. In particular, this book would not have been possible without the guidance and support of Frances Farac. Thank you for making my dream come true.

I would also like to thank my publishers, McGraw-Hill. It has been an absolute pleasure and a privilege dealing with such a dynamic and fun-loving team. Your advice, encouragement and total professionalism have been an inspiration. Thank you for bringing one of my lifelong dreams to reality.

And finally my wife, Felicia Bartolome, a truly wonderful woman. You saw to it that our lives still kept surging forward despite the long hours I spent pursuing my dream. I am truly blessed to have you in my life.

PURCHASING PRACTICES

Cost reduction doesn't just mean the reduction of expenses. You can also achieve greater profits through the more efficient use of the money you spend. By clearly understanding what you are buying, the reasons for buying and the cost, you can avoid wasting money on unnecessary extras. And never, ever assume that you are getting the best deal possible. The following ideas will help you get more bang for your buck.

Chapter 1

Purchasing practices

This chapter covers:

1. Spend only when absolutely required
2. Always ask the price first
3. Ask for a cheaper price
4. Ask for a discount for customer loyalty
5. Get three quotes
6. Keep records of the prices
7. Doing it yourself saves money
8. Be practical about what you buy
9. How many is enough?
10. Buy in bulk
11. Partnership purchases
12. Partners in competition
13. Long-term savings
14. Personally sign all cheques
15. Shop around for a bargain
16. If this were my money … ?
17. Don't spend a cent
18. Is that free delivery really free?
19. Plan your purchasing
20. Make a shopping list
21. When the salesperson comes knocking, let them in
22. When a sale is not a sale
23. Lease versus buy

1.   Spend only when absolutely required

I first started my business from the lounge room of my rented one-bedroom apartment, using a leased computer on the dining table. Back then I was a jack-of-all-trades who used cardboard boxes for filing cabinets and begged, borrowed and recycled everything I needed to ensure my business would be a success. Success to any small business operator is about having a good cash flow. And when you are just starting a business, money may not be coming in as fast as you had hoped—so forgo all the high-tech office equipment, fancy furniture and extra staff. There is plenty of time for those things in the years to come. Remember, a business without all the fancy trimmings is still a viable venture, but a vacant office full of equipment is an auction just waiting to happen.

2.   Always ask the price first

Before you purchase any product or service, always ask for a price or quote first. Recently I needed to have a large perspex poster board taken down from my office wall, and all that was required was to have six screws removed. It was Friday afternoon and things were frantic in the salesroom, so I called the building maintenance guy, who removed the poster in literally two minutes flat. I was ecstatic until I received his invoice for $55. When I queried the bill, he just smiled and informed me that's how much he charges for a job. Despite my protests and attempted negotiations to lower the price he knew there was nothing I could do. So even with a small job, ensure you get a price or quote beforehand.

3.   Ask for a cheaper price

In today's competitive market, companies are forever going out of their way to secure business and keep customers. You should always ask a potential supplier for a better deal than the initial quote. Be sure the cheaper price you have negotiated does not impact on the level and quality of service you receive from the supplier. So go on and ask for a reduction. The worst that can happen is the supplier will say no, but they might also say yes!

4.   Ask for a discount for customer loyalty

If you have been doing regular business with a supplier over a long period of time, consider renegotiating the terms of your contract. A marketing company saved themselves tens of thousands of dollars by renegotiating the credit card merchant fees charged by its bank. The company, which had consistently increased their business with the bank over a number of years, decided it was time to ask for cheaper rates, and it was a good thing they did. Many businesses are finally beginning to realise the true power of a customer's 'lifetime value' and are open to negotiating the price, contractual terms and service requirements.

5.   Get three quotes

As a rule of thumb, you should always get at least three written quotes for all purchases of equipment and supplies. It always pays to compare prices. Ensure that you give each company the same information to quote on; that way you will be comparing apples with apples. You will be stunned at how much the price for the same item can differ from one supplier to the next.

When I was buying my first laptop computer, I made sure that I got three quotes—out of necessity because I knew nothing about computers nor did I know how much I should be paying. The results astounded me. The difference between the cheapest price and the most expensive was around $1500. I finally selected the middle quote that was only $300 more expensive than the cheapest quote, and in doing so, saved over $1000.

6.   Keep records of the prices

My little black book is my greatest resource when it comes to saving my business money. This notebook records the prices of every product I purchase on a regular basis, providing an easy reference guide should I need to compare prices with another supplier. It also enables me to track the frequency and amount of any price increases. My little black book is with me everywhere I go. If I come across a product I am currently using, I always pull out my book and compare prices. I have saved my business, clients and previous employers thousands of dollars this way. And it's all thanks to my little black book.

7. Doing it yourself saves money

Home renovation, car maintenance, gardening, furniture restoration—you name it, you can become a do-it-yourself expert in just about any skill there is. Hundreds of books have been written on the subject, there are numerous courses and qualifications available, and some of you reading this book may even be running a do-it-yourself business. DIY is big business and it can save your business a lot of money. How many things are you paying contractors or service people to do that you could actually be doing yourself? In the earlier poster board example, a screwdriver and five minutes of my time would have saved me over fifty dollars. Before calling in any contractor, consider whether the job can be done in-house. Look at the members of your team. Does anyone have a particular skill in areas outside their current job description? DIY definitely saves money. However, always think about the consequences of your actions and don't attempt anything that could be dangerous to you or your colleagues. Many budding DIY home renovators will do most tasks except for the electrical work—they leave that to a qualified electrician because of the potential dangers involved—and will be happy to use their unsung skills to save your company money.

8. Be practical about what you buy

Don't fall prey to the powers of mass marketing and advertising when choosing your products and supplies. In many cases, there is little difference in the quality of products except for the images and emotions they create in our minds. Don't be fooled by all the smoke and mirrors—it will cost your business money. Consider those adverts where testers unwittingly choose cheap, non-branded products over glamour label goods, and buy your supplies based on their practicality, not on how they look.

One company I worked for had twelve fluorescent green document trays sitting in the storeroom that someone had purchased from a trendy office supplies boutique because they thought they looked really cool. Unfortunately that coolness also cost the company an icy $50 more than the standard grey trays. Not only was money wasted, the trays sat gathering dust in the storeroom because the staff later decided they were not so attractive.

9. How many is enough?

How many items of a particular product do you really need? Stock control is an area where a lot of money can be saved if it is managed well.

Some time ago I inherited an expensive problem when I was employed to manage a new multimillion dollar leisure facility. While taking a tour around the centre on my first day, I walked into the storage room to find enough sporting equipment to last a decade. There were even items purchased for activities that the centre wasn't built to cater for. It turned out that the purchasing manager had been given the responsibility of buying all the stock without much direction as to what was required—so he just went along with the generous budget allocated. Fortunately a refund for some of the goods could be organised with the supplier, saving the centre over $2000.

If you have specific purchasing requirements, such as in the example above, do not leave it solely up to the purchasing or administration staff. They may not have the specific technical knowledge to do the task correctly. As a small business operator, you are ultimately responsible for all purchases, so ensure the person who actually needs the product has a lot of input into what is being bought so that the right product can be purchased at the right price. Further useful tips on inventory control are provided in Chapter 9.

10. Buy in bulk

Buying products in large quantities can offer substantial savings for the small business operator. Many suppliers can provide up to a 30 per cent discount for bulk purchases of some products.

Greg runs his own photography business and is well known for his portraits and wedding photos. The staple supply of his business is photographic film. When Greg was first starting out and money was tight, he was only able to purchase film in small quantities, at inflated prices. Now that his business is booming he is able to purchase film by the hundreds and in doing so, save himself a further 25 per cent on the cost of the film.

However, ensure the savings you make by buying in bulk are not cancelled out by having your money tied up in product that is just sitting in a room taking up valuable storage space or that isn't going to sell. Luckily for Greg, photography film takes up very little storage space; nevertheless, it is important that the film is stored properly and not kept for months and months without use. He normally purchases film to last around two months and then buys another bulk order. Also ensure that any bulk purchase discounts you negotiate with your suppliers do not result in a reduction in the service or quality of goods you receive.

11. Partnership purchases

Are there other businesses that you can team up with to buy supplies in bulk? Most businesses require similar products such as stationery, paper and other office supplies. Your purchasing partners do not have to be in the same industry as you; all the businesses require is a need for the same basic items. By coordinating our purchasing habits between three sales offices, my previous company saved a further $5 per printer toner cartridge. Each office used about twenty cartridges a year resulting in a combined saving of $300.

12. Partners in competition

Don't limit yourself to forming partnerships with non-competing businesses. Your biggest competitor can sometimes become your best ally.

Mary, Wong, Phillip and Annabel all operate food court outlets within a small shopping complex. While the 'Fab Four' are competitors, vying for the business of every person who walks into the food court, they are also very smart business operators. They have banded together and formed a mini cooperative to purchase consumables such as napkins, plastic utensils and disposable coffee cups at a greatly discounted rate from the one supplier. They have a written agreement signed by all participating partners that outlines elements such as who will make the purchase, how the payments and any reimbursements will be made, and how any problems with service or product quality are to be handled. While they are guarded about their success, they have hinted that savings are in the vicinity of 10 to 15 per cent.

Have a look around at your competitors. Are there any opportunities just waiting to be exploited by a cooperative approach?

13.   Long-term savings

If you regularly use a product but can only afford to buy it in small amounts because of limited storage space or a lack of funds, then ask your supplier for a bulk purchasing rate. Most suppliers should agree as long as you commit to purchasing a certain quantity of the product over a specified period of time. This strategy helped me to great effect when I started my business. One of my first products was a self-published manual that I successfully sold to non-profit organisations. I couldn't afford to get thousands of the manuals printed at once so they had to be done in smaller print runs. This resulted in a higher cost of printing, so I negotiated a much lower rate with the printer based on a guaranteed number of publications being required over twelve months. This saved a great deal of money and enabled me to launch my business without having the hefty up-front costs. Always try to negotiate discounts with relevant suppliers for long-term buying commitments.

14.   Personally sign all cheques

Do you sign all cheques yourself and limit the number of people with signing authority to the bare minimum? If not, then why not? This measure of control is guaranteed to provide you with a clear understanding of how your business is spending money, and thereby put you in a better position to control unnecessary expenses. Pay attention to what you are signing. Believe it or not, a huge number of business botch-ups are due to busy owners or managers placing a hurried signature on a contract or cheque without first reading what they are signing. Success is in the detail, and a few seconds to check what you are authorising could save your business a lot of money.

15.   Shop around for a bargain

Don't always go to major suppliers to buy your goods. Try to source smaller establishments that can provide the same product for a much cheaper price. The simplest example of this is purchasing office stationery. Personal experience has shown that you can get much cheaper products from the local $2 shop rather than the major stationery suppliers. Did you ever sit back and wonder who actually pays for all those glossy catalogues, television commercials and newspaper adverts placed by the big chain stores? The customer, of course! There is always a cheaper option to the one you're looking at, and you should try to find it.

> *When I took over the operation of a sales centre in Brisbane, I found the business regularly used couriers to deliver products and pick up customer payments. The previous management were using a big name courier company that charged a big name company price for their services. I spent one morning calling every courier company in the phone book and getting them to send me their rates and service details. I then short-listed five companies and got a representative from each to pay me a visit so I could 'interrogate' them in detail. The end result was a fantastic service from a lesser known courier company. I saved between $7 and $40 per job and their service was first-rate.*

So, before buying anything, remind yourself—there is a cheaper way! Then go out and find it.

16.   If this were my money ... ?

As an alternative to budgeting, ask all your staff to justify everything they spend. As the owner and manager of your business, you must consider every dollar spent as coming out of your own pocket—because it is. Your goal is to have your staff thinking exactly the same way. Have them ask themselves: would I still buy this if I were using my own money? Many businesses also offer a share of the profits to their staff. This allows for a feeling of greater ownership and the money they spend really is theirs.

17.   Don't spend a cent

If you really want to take cost saving to its ultimate level, set aside one month where you do not spend a single cent on any variable costs. Would your business really suffer if it did not purchase any new office supplies, stationery or other one-off expenses for a single month? My guess is a resounding no. I use this strategy in my business once every six months with great success. The key is not to overspend in the period leading up to or after the no-spend month.

18. Is that free delivery really free?

A colleague once told me a great story of how one of his staff purchased ten thousand paper clips so the total invoice amount would qualify for the free delivery offer. While we both had a great laugh over this, it comes with a pretty serious moral. Free delivery is never free if you have to buy a certain dollar amount in order to receive it.

19. Plan your purchasing

My mother always said never shop when you are hungry, because you end up buying more than you really need. The same principle applies in your business. Plan your purchases to ensure that you have adequate supplies.

It was nearly 4 pm on a Friday evening and Tony was printing out 1500 personalised direct mail letters to his customers. They needed to be packed and posted before 6 pm in order to reach the customers by Monday, to coincide with the launch of his promotion. Things were going according to plan until the toner on the printer ran out and there were no spares in the office. It was too late to order toner from his normal supplier, so Tony had to make an expensive dash to the local stationery store and pay $85 more than usual for a new cartridge. Given the importance of the promotion, he decided to purchase a second cartridge just in case he ran out again. Tony's lack of planning cost him an extra $170, plus the extra hassle and stress of having to get the replacement toners.

Planning your purchases in advance avoids you having to buy things out of desperation—when you are hungry—and thereby buying too much, paying too much and purchasing items you don't need.

20. Make a shopping list

Always make a shopping list and stick to it, was another favourite piece of advice from my mother. Regardless of what you are shopping for, prepare a list of everything you need and stick to it. This means you only buy what you need and prevents you forgetting something that could potentially cost you time or money at a later date. And try to avoid catalogue cruising—pulling out the glossy catalogue packed with tempting goodies and letting your senses take control of the purchasing. Before you know it, you've ordered $500 worth of goods you will probably never use—but at least they look good!

21. When the salesperson comes knocking, let them in

We've probably all experienced an unannounced visit or phone call from a salesperson trying to sell us something. I learnt very early on that some of the best deals could be secured from these people. One day a man came knocking on my door trying to sign me to a contract which would provide me with a constant supply of spring water for the office. I had already been using one company for about eight months so I wasn't interested. Yet thankfully, this salesman was extremely persistent and he told me he had a 'great deal' for me. A quick comparison and calculation of prices indicated that I would save $200 a year on drinking water. Since that day I always give salespeople an opportunity to do me a great deal.

22. When a sale is not a sale

Just because an item is on sale doesn't necessarily mean it is a good deal. My wife has a wardrobe full of bargains that were purchased years ago at sales and are yet to see the light of day. Don't be suckered into buying something on impulse just because it is going cheap.

23. Lease versus buy

Small business owners are often faced with an expensive dilemma when it comes to buying necessary office items such as photocopiers, fax machines, furniture and computers. For many businesses, the outright purchase of these items is not an option, and leasing provides a viable alternative. While you do not physically own the items, leasing enables you to continually upgrade your equipment to cater for changes in technology or growth in your business. Leasing also frees up your cash flow, allowing you to invest money in other revenue-generating activities. In many instances, after-sales technical support is also provided as part of the agreement. This book was even written on a leased computer!

24. Lease then buy

If you initially lease equipment and after a while decide you want to buy the product outright, speak to the rental company first. Many companies have a policy whereby you can purchase the rental model direct from them for a much cheaper price. And since the model you are buying is 'used', negotiate a good price to buy it just after they have given it a service. The lease on my computer is due in a few months time. I contacted the leasing agent and discovered that it will only cost me a few hundred dollars to purchase it outright at the end of the lease.

25. Barter to save

To save costs, why not barter your products and services with other companies in exchange for their services?

June has run a printing business for many years and regularly trades her printing services in exchange for goods and services such as clothing, hairdressing, food and restaurant meals. Many of the jobs she does for these businesses are simple in nature and cost her very little by way of time or supplies.

As the popularity of bartering increases, you may also consider joining a barter exchange to put you in contact with other businesses interested in bartering their products and services. But be aware that the value of the bartered goods and services may be taxable, so it is wise to check with your accountant before you begin.

26. Going once, going twice, sold!

Don't waste money buying everything brand spanking new. Auctions are a goldmine of bargains and you are guaranteed to find almost anything you are looking for at only a fraction of the price. Office desks, chairs, computers, filing cabinets, meeting tables, fax machines, printers, fitness equipment, electrical items and whitegoods are just some of the items you can find. Michael, a good friend and successful entrepreneur, completely fitted out his whole office for less than $1000 by going to just one auction.

27. Some other ideas for buying up cheap

Here are some other great ways to find your business a few bargains.

Trade show bargains

If you're in the market for a particular product, look for it at a trade show. Many exhibitors offer special discounts for any order placed at a show. Often they will also discount their display samples to avoid paying to freight them back to their showroom or warehouse. Make sure that you are driving a vehicle big enough to transport the item immediately.

Factory direct purchases

Have a good look at the business you are in and determine if there are any products that you can buy direct from the manufacturer. Cutting out the middleman is a bright idea that will save you a lot of money.

Classified deals

Shop around in the classifieds section of your newspaper or trading post and you will almost always find a bargain. Classifieds are a cost-saving paradise that can be exploited from the comfort of your office.

Garage sales

If there's one happening in your neighbourhood, take a few minutes to drop by and see what you can find. A few years ago I bought a melamine three-drawer filing cabinet for only $20.

28. Cash is king

Wherever possible, accept cash payments from your customers. There are no merchant fees or charges for dealing in cash, other than your own bank fees and charges. Do your maths and work out if it is viable for you to offer a discount to your customers for paying in cash. Alternatively, if a supplier offers a discount for cash payments, then consider taking up this option.

Joe is an electrician and also repairs whitegoods as a side business. By paying cash for any parts he needs Joe receives a 5 per cent discount from his supplier.

Even in this cashless society we live in, cash is still king.

29. Time is money

Some people are happy to travel half an hour to save two dollars on a purchase. There is no point travelling across town to buy something that is going to save you only a few dollars when extra time and petrol costs offset any savings. Your time could be better spent marketing your business, meeting with customers or planning new sales strategies. In business, time is money, so use both of them wisely.

30. Ask for your suppliers' help

Ask your suppliers how they can save you money. Most are happy to help out because it is in their best interests to do so. We all like to do business with people who care about us and our business and who want loyal customers.

Bill owns and operates a small function centre that caters for weddings, birthdays and other such events. One of the biggest maintenance costs every year is the resurfacing of the wooden parquetry floor. The process involves stripping back the coating and reapplying a new surface. Bill used to buy all the raw materials from a supplier and hire a separate contractor to do the job. One day he was talking to the supplier and asked him if there was a cheaper way of doing the resurfacing. His response was music to Bill's ears: 'Sure, you can do it yourself and I'll show you how.' The supplier trained Bill and another of his employees on how to resurface the floor. This saved Bill $2500 a year in maintenance costs.

31. Try before you buy

Many of you will already be using this strategy to increase your sales. Allowing customers to try your product is an excellent way to overcome their hesitancy as it completely removes any risk. Conversely, when it comes to purchasing products and supplies for your own business, look for opportunities to trial products and equipment for free before purchasing them. A large number of businesses will give their customers free samples and free trial offers of their products and services.

Andy had read a lot of information about the benefits of having a business coach who could work with him on developing his fledgling handyman business into a successful enterprise. However, Andy was a little sceptical about the whole concept of having a coach for his business and he didn't want to commit to someone without first seeing what they were like. He met with five different coaches who offered a no-risk complimentary trial session before finding the person he really clicked with. Many coaches charge upwards of $200 per session so Andy was able to save himself in excess of $1000 to find the right person.

What can you try for free before purchasing it? Even if suppliers aren't offering free trial periods and samples, try asking them anyway. In this current climate businesses are pulling out all stops to get new customers and it would be a rare occasion that you wouldn't be able to negotiate some form of free deal.

32. Beware hidden running costs

Before you purchase any piece of office equipment, technology or machinery, research the cost of the consumable items they use such as toner cartridges and batteries. If you only compare based on the purchase price, cheaper is not always cheapest. Take a look at the following example and you'll see what I mean.

Harry wanted to buy a photocopier for his office and had narrowed the choices down to two models. Model A would cost him $1000 while Model B was $1400. Both copiers provided much the same functions and reliability so Model A seemed like the better deal. That was until Harry compared the price of replacing the toner cartridges in each copier. The toner for Model A cost $80 each and would need to be replaced every month, while Printer B cartridges were only $60 and would last for up to two months. Harry did the maths and his calculations for a twelve-month period were as follows:

Model A:
purchase price $1000 + toner costs ($80 x 12) = $1960

Model B:
purchase price $1400 + toner costs ($60 x 6) = $1760

As this example shows, one model may at first seem cheaper than the other, but once the cost of consumables are factored into the equation, the more expensive model may end up being the more cost-effective alternative.

2

STAFFING

Payroll is one of the largest expense items for most businesses and normally the first area targeted when looking to cut costs. Unfortunately, most businesses take the approach of the wholesale slash and burn of employees. Mass retrenchments and redundancies are a common occurrence. While this approach may save your business money in the immediate short term, there are few medium to longer term benefits to be gained. The good news is you can still reduce your payroll bill significantly with a bit of thought and planning.

Chapter 2

Staffing

This chapter covers:

Recruitment

Reorganising, restructuring and reducing staff

Outsourcing for savings

Recruitment

The cost of finding staff for your business can increase the strain on your cash flow. But it doesn't have to be that way. The following strategies can be easily implemented to not only save you money but also ensure you get the right person for the job!

33. Replacing staff

When an employee leaves your business, use this as an opportunity to save money. Before you race off to put an advert in the employment section of the paper, sit down and evaluate if you really need to replace the person and keep the position, or whether the tasks can be divided among other staff or done away with altogether.

Julie manages a marketing firm and she had until recently employed a full-time person to generate leads for her sales staff to contact. One day the leads coordinator resigned, leaving Julie with a big decision to make. She made a few phone calls to list brokers and got the price of purchasing specific segmented lists. She discovered that the total cost of purchasing a set quantity of leads from a broker was $9000 cheaper than the annual cost of employing the leads coordinator to provide the same number of contacts.

So, don't rehire just because a position has become vacant.

34. Hire internally

If a position becomes available and it does need to be filled, first look for a replacement from within your current employees. Not only is this a great way to reward valued employees, it also ensures that they don't go and work for your competitor.

Chris is the Vice President of Operations for an international sales and marketing firm. He began his career with the company over ten years ago as a salesperson. After showing much promise he was given the opportunity to further his skills and experience in an administrative role at one of their busy sales offices. He was then placed on a manager trainee program where he developed the necessary skills to become a fully-fledged sales manager. After a number of years of success, he was promoted to an operations role and from there moved into his current post as VP.

Chris's company has kept a loyal and valued employee for well over a decade, while also saving themselves a great deal of money on advertising and recruitment.

35. Get it right the first time

If you are recruiting for a senior position within your business, make sure you do it right the first time round. A colleague was telling me how their company recently hired a person for a senior management position. After the interview the new employee spent an initial four weeks in training and was then flown interstate and put up in an apartment to complete the second half of their training—all at the company's expense. During the initial weeks of training they had experienced problems with their pay, a lack of communication with their supervisor and conflicting messages regarding the actual length and format of the training. Before the training was complete the new employee resigned to take up a position with another company. Taking into account recruitment and training costs, airfares and accommodation, my colleague's company had spent in the vicinity of $10 000, only to come up empty-handed. Get it right the first time by ensuring everything is clearly explained and by presenting a consistent and professional image, so the new employee is excited about working for their new company. Remember, you only get one chance at a first impression.

36. Jobs on the Net

If you have an ongoing need for staff, use modern technology to help with your recruitment efforts. There are a number of job search websites where you can advertise vacant positions, such as www.SEEK.com.au. For less than $100 per month, you can put your job ad in front of hundreds of thousands of candidates around the country; plus, SEEK takes your ad to the relevant candidates. Over half a million people have requested to be emailed as soon as suitable vacancies in their job area are listed.

> *Call centres have become one of the boom industries of the new millennium. Unfortunately though, an occupational hazard for any business owner in this industry is the high turnover of staff. Glen operates a small call centre in the heart of the city and was regularly finding himself short on staff. However, the cost of advertising in the newspaper was proving to be far greater than what he had initially budgeted for recruitment. Glen heard about advertising on SEEK through a friend and decided to give it a go. He hasn't looked back and has managed to maintain a full team of staff ever since. By advertising on the Internet, Glen is constantly receiving applications via email or over the phone. Rather than having to undertake large, expensive and time-consuming recruitments, Glen is able to employ small groups of two or three people at a time.*

For a small monthly fee your advert works 24/7, providing you with a regular stream of potential new staff.

37. Referred staff

You can save on recruitment costs by encouraging your employees to refer potential staff members to your business. A referral from an existing employee doesn't guarantee they get the job—nepotism costs you money—as they still have to be interviewed by you. By offering an incentive for staff to refer potential employees, you will certainly increase the level of participation.

> *The sales industry has a very high turnover of part-time and casual staff. I used to offer an incentive to my employees to refer friends and associates to me for the many positions we had available. If I employed one of these people and they were able to make a set number of sales in three weeks, the referrer would receive a $100 bonus in their pay packet. This was a very successful strategy, as it turned out to be much cheaper than advertising in the paper and I only paid up if the person turned out to be a good performing employee. It doesn't just apply to casual positions—one company employs the same recruitment strategy for their mid-level management positions. If the applicant successfully completes the two-month training program and the first three months on the job, the referring employee receives a $1000 reward.*

38. Recruitment savings from others' misfortune

Keep track of businesses similar to yours that may be announcing plans to downsize or completely close their operations. These businesses will be freeing up qualified and experienced people who will no doubt be looking for work. And the great part is that you don't need to provide much training as they already have the experience.

Apart from owning a fast food franchise, Jenny owns a small chain of thriving hairdressing salons. She is a highly astute businesswoman as well as being great with a pair of scissors. I remember her telling me how over three hundred hairdressing salons had closed down over a twelve-month period—she mainly put this down to the owners being good hairdressers but poor business people. I asked her whether these frightening figures concerned her and in true style she proceeded to describe how she had opened two new salons at the same time that her competitors were going under, and she hadn't paid a cent for recruiting or training experienced and qualified staff, all of whom brought with them a ready-made list of loyal clients. Having heard that some salons were about to close, Jenny had paid a visit to a number of well-known and respected staff to offer them jobs. Of course they jumped at the opportunity, knowing full well they would be on the market in a few weeks time.

Remember, in business one person's loss is another's opportunity. So keep your eyes and ears open and save big on your recruitment and training costs.

39. Hire multiskilled staff

When looking through applicants' resumes, pay particular attention to people who have skills or experience in areas other than the position they are applying for. If they are suitable for the position, their added skills will be a bonus to your organisation and will provide them with an excellent opportunity for advancement.

One of the best salespeople I ever employed also had a strong background in computers and IT. Shane's extra skills came in very handy when we were experiencing small glitches or when it came to advice on what sort of new equipment to purchase. He saved us a few thousand dollars on service calls we never had to make and on

> *purchasing the right equipment. He was happy to help out as he gained a great sense of self-satisfaction from being the 'fixer' and having those extra responsibilities when any problems arose.*

By employing people with multiple skills, you will reap the reward of reducing the size of your workforce and avoiding the expensive one-off service of contractors and consultants.

40. Some more low-cost strategies

Some of the cheapest and most effective recruitment strategies I have ever implemented were also some of the simplest. As the saying goes, the simplest things in life are often the best! Here are a few simple ideas that have saved me thousands of dollars in recruitment costs and resulted in the employment of some of my best staff.

Poster in your shop/business window

This is a tried and tested idea that will cost you literally nothing. Make it presentable by producing something on your PC rather than a note scrawled in handwriting.

Public noticeboards

Use the same notice that you put up in the window of your business, and place it on the public noticeboards at the local library, university or TAFE college, supermarkets, leisure centres and doctors' surgeries.

Employment centres

A quick telephone call to your social services department should provide you with a list of local employment agencies that will refer applicants to your business for free. I have employed some outstanding staff who had been referred from these organisations and it hasn't cost me a cent.

Backpackers hostels

If your business requires casual and part-time staff, look no further than the backpacker hostels and Youth Hostel Association offices. Place an advert on the noticeboard and hear the phone ring off the hook. In my experience, travellers make great employees as they are hard workers, generally really fun people and are willing to give any job a go to earn a few extra dollars.

The downside of employing travellers is that they rarely stay on longer than a few months, often due to visa restrictions. However, if you are a good employer then the backpacker grapevine will provide you with your very own staff referral program. I have had people call me for work through bumping into someone who used to work for me. Too easy!

Classified adverts

If you do advertise in the newspaper, consider using line ads or classified ads rather than the large display adverts. Apart from saving your business hundreds of dollars, many papers run promotions where for $10 more you can either get an extra ad in the following week's edition or be placed on their Internet employment site.

Local papers

If you operate a small local business, don't waste your money placing an ad in the major newspapers. Advertising in the local community newspaper is far cheaper and it targets potential employees who live in the area. There is nothing worse than speaking to a potential applicant who is just the person you are looking for, only to hear that your workplace is too far for them to travel.

Reorganising, restructuring and reducing staff

Can you do things differently from how you are doing them now? Just by changing the way you structure your business can lead to huge savings in your staffing costs. The ideas presented will help reduce your payroll without affecting your ability to run your business.

41. Job-sharing can work

There are many people in the workforce who would prefer to work part-time and have excellent skills in areas where it might be difficult to hire quality people. One way of overcoming this dilemma and at the same time saving money is to allow two (or possibly more people) to do the one job. Two people are more flexible than one, so during periods of high demand they can work together to ensure deadlines are met. Alternatively, when times are slow it may be possible to cut these employees' hours, further reducing your expenses.

While studying at university, I took on a job-share position as a youth worker at the local youth centre. Louise was my job-share buddy and we complemented each other extremely well. By her own admission Louise couldn't organise a hangover in a brewery, but she had the energy and vitality of an Energiser Bunny. So I managed the youth centre and she managed the young people. The job-sharing worked perfectly as we were able to fit our work in and around our classes. The youth centre also benefited as it reduced its staffing levels from one and a half positions to one full-time job-share position. The money it saved on staffing was poured back into worthwhile programs and resources for the young people.

This example shows how two people in one post may bring additional skills and experience to your business. Plus, if one person is off sick or on leave then the other person can usually cover for them. Job-sharing can also work extremely well for highly stressful positions or those involving highly repetitive tasks.

Data entry must be one of the most repetitive and brain-numbing jobs there is: sitting all day in front of the computer, pounding away at the keyboard entering thousands of names, numbers and address details. Michael originally employed one full-time data entry person for his marketing company but he found that their productivity waned towards the latter half of each day as they became tired and bored. As a result, the amount of data entered in the morning shift compared to the afternoon shift was almost 2:1. Eventually his employee left, so Michael decided to turn the position into a job-share and employed two part-time staff to work half a day each. The result was a large increase in productivity from two employees who left each day still full of energy.

Job-sharing may also allow your business to keep a valued employee who is able to work only part-time. While it doesn't work for all positions, job-sharing can prove an ideal alternative with some. Plus, you might find you can hire better employees, increase productivity, save money and end up with happier staff in those positions.

42. Use casual employees and save

Your business may benefit by employing casual staff. Even though you tend to pay a higher hourly rate for casuals, your payroll and administrative expenses can be substantially reduced by not having to provide sick pay, public holidays and annual leave.

Sonya recently started a promotions company, providing staff for many major events and promotional campaigns. As part of her business plan, she calculated the potential costs of employing staff as both casual and permanent part-time employees. By bringing most staff on as casual employees, she would realise a saving of over $15 000 in payroll and administration costs per annum.

Casual employment provides flexibility for both employer and employees and, if used effectively, can keep your payroll costs under control.

43. Do you have too many people?

Many businesses find themselves having to support a payroll that is far bigger than their business requires. In most cases this situation has evolved due to the following reasons:

- the inability of management to hire the right people and to get rid of those who just aren't working out

- poor productivity and the hiring of more people in an attempt to compensate

- a lack of automation and technology, resulting in more staff being required

- managers employing more staff than necessary to give a false sense of importance and status for them and their department. (Have you heard of the term 'empire building'?)

Have a look at your processes and your people and determine to what extent this has occurred in your business. Before hiring new staff ask yourself the following questions:

- Are existing staff working to full capacity?

- Can staff be multiskilled?

- Are there any positions that can be changed from full-time to part-time?

- Can certain functions be outsourced?

- Can changes be made to systems and processes to improve productivity?

- Will installing new technology reduce the need for certain staff?

I learned a great deal about human resource management from a very talented HR manager by the name of Leonie. One of the first things she told me was, 'A good boss realises that to hire a person you must first have a worthwhile job for them to do that no one else in your business or no piece of machinery can do better, faster or cheaper'. Certainly an excellent piece of advice that will ensure you never have more employees than you actually need.

Hire people only when necessary and regularly evaluate whether you need all the people you have on your payroll. Don't be afraid to consider the fact that you have too many people and act on it.

44. Executive Director of Special Projects and Corporate Fiscal Liaison

Some business owners fall into the trap of creating unnecessary positions with fancy (but meaningless) job titles to help out a friend or a friend of a friend! I have experienced first-hand many situations where a business operator has hired a relation or close friend to a newly developed position within their company in order to help this person out of a tight spot, only to have it backfire on them. It's a fact—nepotism costs you money, so don't do it!

Another classic case is where an employee is not doing their current job effectively and rather than terminate them, a new job is created and the employee is moved into that new position. I have worked in a number of companies where this has become standard operating procedure. This sends a very strong message to all employees to be as unproductive and as inefficient as possible and hell, you'll probably get yourself a promotion and a pay rise because of it.

Remember—business is business. End of story! As soon as you start creating positions that your business doesn't actually need and definitely can't afford just to help someone out of a jam, then prepare yourself for a whole pile of torment. Hiring people you know well isn't a problem as long as they have the necessary skills and experience and they're the best candidate for the job.

45. Too many chiefs and not enough Indians

This is a well-known phrase used for organisations that have too many managers and executives sitting around making decisions (generally bad ones) and not enough people to actually do all the work. Apart from having a huge impact on your payroll, excessive layers of management generally result in slow and cumbersome decision-making as everyone wants to have their say on every small issue in order to justify their existence. If your business has too many layers of management, it makes sense to make changes.

Rather than retrenching excess staff, take a more positive approach and make middle managers more accountable to your bottom line by:

- getting them to generate new business for the company by making sales calls and utilising both their personal and their professional networks

- having them develop a proposal as to how your business could cut costs or increase revenue

- having them visit every client with the aim of getting specific feedback on how well your company is meeting their needs

- retraining them to take on other tasks such as training

- transferring them to another section of your business

- adopting any of the ideas in this book and have them see it through to completion.

46. How many is too many?

Don't roster on too many staff during periods when business is slow. I know this sounds straightforward but just take a walk into any shopping centre an hour before closing time and you can see three or four staff standing around in most stores having a chat without a customer in sight. Are there opportunities for your business to reduce staffing levels during quieter periods of the day, week, month or year?

Bill runs a thriving souvenir and novelty shop in the heart of the city. Every day Bill personally opens the store at 9 am to catch any early morning trade and he is the only person on duty until 11 am. From 11.15 am onwards a steady procession of tour buses park outside his store so a part-time employee helps out until 4 pm. If things get really busy, Bill makes a quick call to his wife to join them and lend a hand. Bill is then alone again until his 6 pm closing. His staffing levels are altered even further during the quieter months of winter. By organising his staffing levels around the ebb and flow of his customers, Bill has reduced his payroll by $15 000 a year.

And are there parts of your business that you can temporarily close during quiet times to reduce the number of staff you need on duty and therefore reduce your payroll expenses?

During non-peak periods the operators of my local train station close all but two of the entry/exit areas, thereby reducing the number of rail staff required on duty. My local fitness centre adopts a similar approach for some of its services when it opens on Sundays. While the gym is fully functioning, the café area is closed due to the lack of business it receives. The gym not only cuts its payroll by not having to employ someone to manage the café, it also saves on power and food costs.

Rather than temporarily close parts of your business, can you combine some of your services into the one service area?

This strategy has been used to great effect by many public swimming pools, which are now run like a small business. Through good planning and design they have combined the reception, cashier, kiosk/cafe and sports shop all around one central service area. So if you want to pay to enter the pool, buy a juice, inquire about swim classes or get yourself a new pair of swim goggles then you go to the same counter. During low periods, only one staff member is required to successfully control all these functions. Aside from the obvious savings in payroll, this also reduces the space needed for extra cashier points (space that can now be used in other ways), and only one cash register is required.

Once you have finished reviewing your staffing levels, take a good hard look at your operating hours. Can your hours of business be reduced without adversely affecting your business?

> One manager of a call centre reduced the shift times from four hours to three and three-quarter hours. While this might not sound like a huge saving, fifteen minutes multiplied by ten employees working two shifts a day, five days a week over forty-eight weeks produced a saving of $14 000 a year. And it had little effect on sales—the shorter time period created greater urgency in the consultants and they became more productive because they had to meet the same targets within less time.

47. Get your customers to do it themselves

Chapter 1 highlighted the cost-saving benefits to your business by doing many things yourself. Well, by applying the same do-it-yourself approach for your customers you can continue to increase your cost-saving opportunities. By making parts of your business self-service, you can reduce your staffing overheads and increase productivity.

> The Make Your Own (MYO) lunch bars have made the self-service philosophy the central component of their winning formula. Customers literally make their own sandwiches or salads from the wide selection of food set out in a variety of buffet style serving areas. At any one time up to twenty people could be making their lunch, just the way they like it. Imagine the number of staff you would have to employ to cater for that sort of demand. A self-service strategy dramatically reduces the number of staff required.

Technology has played a major part in increasing our reliance on self-service and reducing payroll costs.

> Jim drives his car to the train station and buys a parking ticket from the ticket machine. He then purchases a train ticket from another ticket machine. He walks up to the relevant gate and inserts his ticket into yet another machine that allows him access to the station platform. While waiting for his train, he pops a few coins in a

vending machine and out drops a steaming hot cup of coffee. He then puts a few more coins into another machine and takes a copy of the daily newspaper to read on his journey to the office. Jim's day has just begun and he has already completed five transactions—with not one 'employee' involved.

Many businesses are harnessing the benefits of technology to make their operations more efficient and cost-effective. As seen in the above example, even the simplest everyday activities can capitalise on technological advances. As highlighted throughout this book, every decision your business makes to improve its bottom line will have certain consequences; introducing new technology into your organisation is no exception. The important factor here is to consider all possible consequences to ensure your final decision is an informed one. Further cost-saving benefits of technology are provided in Chapter 7.

48. Telecommuting

Telecommuting can prove to be a cost-saving winner for many businesses. With the increase in technology it is now both practical and cost-effective to bring the job to the person rather than the person to the job. This is particularly true for occupations that rely heavily on the use of computers, the Internet, phones and fax.

By having employees working at their own personal peak times and from the comfort of their home, the opportunity exists to increase productivity and decrease absenteeism. Employees are able to work in spite of minor illness, car trouble, household emergencies and public transport delays—situations that traditionally may have prevented them from coming to work or at least delayed them significantly. Telecommuting also allows them to coordinate their work schedules with personal demands, giving them increased flexibility and a greater sense of freedom and personal control.

Telecommuting has been used to great effect in Amanda's financial planning business. Her team of six financial consultants all work from their home offices that Amanda has set up with laptop computers and Internet and fax facilities. The staff meet two mornings a week in Amanda's office to review their progress and discuss strategies and new business opportunities. By having her employees work from home, Amanda has saved a great deal on office rental and administration staff, enabling her to lease a small serviced office in a more prestigious building. The meeting room facilities are free and the upmarket address gives her small company a marketable identity that she couldn't otherwise afford. Amanda has also found her staff to be more productive as they are able to coordinate the erratic hours of a financial planner without detriment to their personal lives.

49. Staff productivity

Are your employees working to their maximum capacity? To find out, evaluate your current methods of operation with a view to increasing the productivity of all your staff. Set performance standards clearly outlining the required duties to be achieved within an allocated time period.

Here are some performance standards a friend of mine sets out for employees working in her busy call centre.

- leads coordinator must generate 250 fresh leads per shift

- data entry staff must enter 400 leads per shift

- sales consultants must make 50 contact calls per shift

- sales consultants must make at least one sale per shift

- office manager must process all sales and enter all new customers into database by the end of each day.

If these performance standards are regularly achieved, my friend knows that her business is operating smoothly. These clearly defined standards are openly communicated to employees in the recruitment process and are attached to job descriptions. The standards are also referred to on a regular basis throughout the working week. Since introducing these standards my friend has avoided the need to have employees work overtime to achieve the same results.

It is often more difficult to quantify such standards in an office environment, where many small business operators find themselves on a daily basis. Defining what will make you and your employees more productive is a personal matter, as only you know the things that need to be done to get the most out of every single day. However, you can apply specific performance standards in these general areas:

Dress code

Your business may have a specific uniform that is required to be worn at all times, or an acceptable level of business wear. You can set standards for general neatness and grooming.

Punctuality

Are there set arrival and departure times for your business? Do you provide set breaks for staff and are these timed?

Reporting procedures

Deadlines for the submission of reports—daily, weekly or monthly—should always be met.

Customer service

Many businesses set customer service standards, such as answering the telephone within three rings, greeting customers in a certain way, or guaranteeing delivery within a given time frame.

50. Punctual savings

Do you have part-time or casual employees who turn up to work late? And do you deduct this time from their pay, even if it is only fifteen minutes? Let me do some quick maths for you to demonstrate how much you can save on wages by making deductions for lateness.

Over the course of one week you could possibly expect ten of your employees to either turn up late or leave early by fifteen minutes once each. This equates to 150 minutes per week or 2½ hours. If the average hourly rate is $15 per hour, this equals approximately $1950 per year in savings. And that is just a conservative estimate.

The bottom line is—if they are not there, they shouldn't get paid. At the very least they should work back to make up for any time lost. Just to be on the safe side, I encourage you to check your local labour laws and employee awards before withholding any pay.

51. A clean saving

Keeping a clean and tidy business is a must. But before you go out and employ your own cleaners or a private contracting firm, consider the following ways to do the cleaning yourself.

Make cleaning part of everyone's job description

Look at fast food chains; they don't employ specific cleaners. Every member of staff pitches in to help empty trays, clean tables and mop floors while the kitchen staff are responsible for keeping their area spick and span.

Lead the way

If staff see managers rolling up their sleeves, they'll be more likely to follow suit.

Make cleaning duties fun

You could organise a roster system so that everyone pitches in to do the vacuuming and empty the bins, or you could have an award for the silliest thing said or done by an employee in the previous week. Their 'prize' is to vacuum the floor for a week.

Provide plenty of rubbish bins

One of the main reasons many businesses have rubbish lying around is because staff and customers have nowhere to put it other than on the floor.

Get your customers involved!

The indoor basketball centre where I go to shoot some hoops has a very novel approach to reducing their cleaning costs. Firstly, all players are requested to wipe their trainers on a large mat prior to entering the court. Secondly, before any group is allowed onto the court they are required to sweep the playing surface using the large pair of scissor brooms left by the side of the court. We never complain because we all know it is for our own good—no one wants to twist an ankle on a dusty floor.

> Gary ran a small sales office and decided to reduce overheads by buying a vacuum cleaner for $40 and doing the cleaning himself. When the staff that arrived early saw him doing this they offered to help which he gratefully accepted. The word soon spread and before long the staff had drawn up a roster to do the vacuuming every

morning. Prior to this, the program had contracted a private cleaner to clean the sales room three times a week at a cost of $225 per month. Gary and his team now do it themselves and it costs them nothing, saving his business around $2700 per year.

52. Job descriptions save you money

Do all of your staff have job descriptions? If not, they should. A job description gives employees a very clear plan of what is expected of them in terms of their roles and responsibilities. A good job description will also include relevant performance standards as an addendum.

53. When times get real tough

Sometimes things don't go as well with our business as we would have hoped. Clients delay purchases, suppliers raise prices, competitors steal market share or the economy goes downhill. Suddenly there's not enough cash coming in and the pressure quickly mounts to do something. Unfortunately, the wholesale reduction of the workforce has become an automatic response for many businesses. In most cases the costs of staff layoffs, such as low morale of remaining staff, reduction in customer service and decreased productivity, generally outweigh any savings to the payroll. Here are some ideas that will have the least negative impact on your business.

Reduce payroll with time off

When it's imperative to temporarily reduce payroll levels, let employees volunteer to take time off for a sabbatical. Due to the damage to morale, firing staff should be the last option. When the economy or business snaps back you will be happy to have seasoned, trained employees ready to return. There are many reasons why your employees may welcome a chance to take unpaid time off with the prospect of coming back when business is on the mend. These may include spending time with their young family, undertaking further study or gaining experience working in a related field.

Introduce a four-day week

During tough times, getting paid for four days is better than not having a job at all because the business has closed down. You will need to sit down and rework your roster to make sure your business is still providing customers with the service they require—but it can be done.

Take your leave

Encourage your employees to take any outstanding annual leave still owing to them. As your business should have already set aside the funds to cover their leave entitlements, there will be no further drain on company funds to cover their wages while they are away.

Don't replace staff when they leave

During good times and bad, employees will move on to other things. When they do, don't replace them. Let natural attrition save you money. Transfer an existing staff member to take on their position or divide their responsibilities.

Make pay cuts

I was based in Malaysia during the economic crisis of the late 1990s, when all employees in my company took a pay cut. It was 10 to 15 per cent for executives and a 5 per cent cut for rank and file employees. While no one liked the cuts it was better than losing our jobs altogether, which was becoming commonplace in many other businesses.

Restructure

As previously mentioned, take a long, hard look at your business and see whether there are any components of your operation that can be completely closed, operating hours changed or functions altered to a self-service style operation.

Retrain staff

Look for opportunities to alter the structure of your company and retrain some of your employees to take on unfamiliar duties. One hotel retrained all back of house staff (sales, marketing, finance, human resources and the like) so they could assist with housekeeping duties and serving in the restaurants during the rare busy periods of an economic and tourism slump.

Outsourcing for savings

Does your business employ people or have departments that are not part of your core activities—travel

departments, caterers, taxation specialists, cleaners, auditors? The cost of having these activities run in-house may be costing you more than if you outsource them to a third party.

54. Use temps during surges

Instead of hiring permanent staff, support your team with temporary workers during peak periods or staff shortages. The temp industry is now very sophisticated, enabling you to quickly access personnel with relevant experience and qualifications in almost any skill area.

The hospitality industry relies heavily on temporary workers. Julie manages a catering business in partnership with her sister. They have a number of permanent part-time staff that assist with their regular functions. Once in a while the company secures a large event that requires a bigger workforce, so Julie turns to temporary staff to support her existing team. A quick call to a temp agency and she has all the experienced staff she needs to get the job done well. By using temps Julie is able to keep her payroll costs to a minimum, and when extra staff are required the cost is factored into her charges to the customer.

55. Outsource to save on staff costs

In many cases, it makes more sense to outsource some of the functions required to successfully operate your business, rather than take on the added responsibility and cost of employing a permanent member of staff. Most small businesses already use a form of outsourcing without even realising it. Your accountant or bookkeeper provides a service to your business for a negotiated fee. I believe successful small businesses are built on having good marketers and managers and the financial aspects should be left to those who really know what they are doing. Rather than struggle to balance the books, I prefer to use my time growing my business by marketing and managing.

Outsourcing certain functions also reduces your need to purchase the associated equipment and consumable items, thereby saving money. For instance, payroll savings are not the only benefit Jenny enjoys by outsourcing her cleaning to a contract cleaning firm. She also saves by not having to buy vacuum cleaners, brooms, cleaning chemicals and garbage bags, nor provide the appropriate storage space.

Many businesses can benefit from the lower overall costs gained by having an external operation perform certain tasks. This was certainly the case for a direct marketing company that distributed over one thousand packages each week to its customers. Due to the growth in their business, a decision was made to move the packaging and distribution of their product to an external mailing house. The direct marketing company could now have its product packed and distributed for 50c cheaper per item, giving them a saving of around $26 000 per annum in wages. This did not include the further saving made by releasing office space previously used for storage and packaging, that could now be used to house their expanding sales and marketing department.

In many cases, outsourcing enables your business to operate at a bare bones level and to optimise the use of your personnel, cash, space and time.

56. Hire a consultant

Although there is a cost associated with bringing in outside consultants, there are times when it makes perfect business sense to do so. Good consultants can help you take a step back and look at your business objectively; however, they should only be used to bring a level of experience and expertise into your business that doesn't already exist and cannot be obtained from other sources.

Consider the following when you are looking at selecting a consultant.

■ Find a consultant that has been used by similar businesses to yours.

■ Be careful when hiring a consultant—remember, you get what you pay for.

■ Learn how to assimilate consultants into your company. A consultant should become part of your existing team and work alongside your employees. Avoid the development of an 'us versus them' mentality.

■ Don't forget to implement their recommendations as given—you're not paying all that money only to have the report sit on your bookshelf gathering dust.

■ Always check the outcomes.

57. Budding professionals

Here's an idea to get your business thousands of dollars' worth of free consultancy. Simply contact your local universities and colleges for student assistance. Most students are required to complete a certain number of hours of practical work experience per semester or undertake a specific project within the community that is relevant to their course. They have the opportunity to gain hands-on experience and a professional reference; you get eager part-time assistance at little or no cost. As part of their thesis or course assessment, many students are required to develop a marketing or business plan for your business.

A well-known community college offers small to medium-sized businesses the opportunity to get a free marketing plan and promotional advice from the college's marketing students. Businesses that partner with the college in this project have a team of marketing students look at all aspects of their business and develop a thorough marketing analysis and plan. The students are often professionals working in their own business and the marketing plan is part of their final course assessment.

There are several other ways to use students' talents to build your business.

- Graphic design students can develop your business logo, letterhead, business card and promotional brochure.

- IT students can design a website for your business or provide expertise to improve your existing site.

- Advertising students can develop an advertising campaign.

- Photography students can take photographs of your business, products and services to be used in future advertising, brochures, website and other promotional strategies.

- Business students can develop a business plan for you.

- Finance students can implement an accounting system for your small business.

58. Outsource your payroll

Small businesses are particularly vulnerable to payroll errors, as most do not have an experienced payroll officer. The legislation surrounding industrial relations, superannuation and workers compensation is extremely complex for the uninitiated and barely manageable for the well-qualified. The concern for every small business is the costly errors that occur daily as business owners battle to calculate correctly the relevant entitlements each employee is due.

Many employers I have spoken to have incorrectly calculated the annual leave of staff that have changed working hours or received pay increases. Many small businesses employ contractors that should be classified as employees. And I heard of one organisation that incorrectly calculated the termination payments of two employees by overpaying them a total of $1500. Incorrect calculations can be an expensive exercise for any business. Once you've paid the money it becomes a very difficult and costly exercise to try to get it back. Conversely, if you underpay your staff then you will be liable for the restitution of these funds. And these examples are just the tip of the iceberg.

The answer for many small businesses is to outsource all their payroll requirements to an experienced payroll company. They can come in and help your business establish appropriate payroll procedures, as well as providing training and ongoing support to you or your staff. Alternatively, you can outsource the complete operation of your payroll services to the company and they will handle everything for you.

Many small businesses are losing significant amounts of money due to incorrect payroll procedures and ill-qualified personnel. Don't let your business be one of them. Get the professionals in and save your business the time, money and stress inherent to this area.

Safety for savings' sake

Compensation claims, increased insurance premiums, low morale and additional staffing costs are just some of the expenses your business will incur from being an unsafe workplace. Don't fall into the trap of believing workplace accidents only happen in factories and on

building sites. Remember, prevention is better than cure, so avoid workplace accidents by creating a safe working environment for your staff. Here are some cost-effective ideas for you to keep a safe workplace.

59. Prevent workplace hazards

Take a proactive approach to preventing workplace accidents by identifying potential problem areas in your business. Working collectively with your employees, draft a list of probable safety hazards that may put you and your staff at risk. Then train your employees to take the necessary precautions so these safety threats don't happen and, where possible, implement appropriate strategies to further reduce the risk of injury.

The following are some potential hazards of a standard office environment:

- Non-ergonomic furniture—office chairs, desks and computer tables

- Trip hazards—telephone and electrical cables not taped down or covered; floor surfaces such as carpet and parquetry tiles not secured flush to the floor; objects left lying around in high traffic areas

- Overloaded power boards—too many electrical items operating from the same power outlet

- Frayed electrical cords—replace all worn or broken electrical cords

- Lifting of objects—use correct posture and lifting techniques

- Storage—correctly label and store objects, especially heavy items

- Unsafe practices—an employee standing on an unstable office chair to change a light bulb

- Unhygienic practices—leaving cups and spoons unwashed; irregular disposal of office litter bins

Romero is a skilled craftsman and operates a furniture restoration business. He employs one full-time craftsman and two apprentices. A key part of their apprenticeship is having a complete understanding of creating a safe workplace. Romero spent two full days explaining how they could anticipate, correct and avoid unsafe work practices. Together, they then developed a checklist of unsafe practices specific to their restoration business. This information was put up in the workshop and included in the staff orientation program.

60. Implement a safety program

If your business fails to take adequate measures to protect your employees while they're on the job, you're creating potential for costly time off and skyrocketing workers compensation premiums. You should take safety seriously and develop a comprehensive awareness, training and management program for your business. Create an expectation among your employees that they will work in a safe manner and strive to create a safe environment. Here are some strategies you can implement immediately.

- Hold periodic safety seminars to remind employees about precautions such as proper lifting techniques and ergonomics.

- Appoint a safety officer, whose responsibility is to identify safety hazards and educate new employees regarding safety procedures.

- Place safety posters around your workplace and reminders in staff newsletters, or circulate emails on different safety issues.

- Introduce staff awards for safety.

You must be keenly aware of all the potential dangers and provide employees with clear direction about safety issues. And you must make employees accountable for actions that could compromise their own safety and the safety of others. But don't spend time, money and resources setting up safety programs only to let them lose momentum. Keep promoting and improving your workplace safety initiatives. Review them regularly and maintain ongoing communication between you and your employees.

61. Some safety tips

These factors all contribute to a safe workplace.

Good ergonomics

There are plenty of inexpensive office chairs, computer tables and keyboards available that comply to OH&S standards, to prevent repetitive motion injuries. Encourage your employees to take quick exercise breaks to stretch their limbs. In our call centres we get staff to stand up and sell for a while.

We provide them with ergonomic chairs and headsets so they can freely move around.

Safe storage

Ensure that all objects are correctly stored to avoid any mishaps. A colleague informed me of several cases where heavy items stored on top shelves and heavy stacked boxes have fallen on people (herself included). I can also recall a friend being injured at work when he lifted a box containing paint tins, but unfortunately the bottom of the box had rotted from moisture and the heavy tins fell on his feet. Although he was wearing shoes he still suffered a broken toe.

No to drugs and alcohol

Either one of these or a combination of both guarantees your business will incur some form of worker accident. This is especially prevalent where employees are working with machinery.

Safe driving

If an employee is injured while driving to, from or during work, your business is most likely liable to cover them under workers compensation. Add to this the cost of repairs to vehicles and the effect on your insurance premiums, and it makes sense to promote safe and sensible driving.

Safety devices

Safety glasses, gloves, harnesses, hard hats, work boots and face masks—if they prevent injury in the workplace, make sure your employees always use them.

Defect repairs

Ensure a safe workplace by keeping electrical wiring, stairways, carpeting, flooring, elevators and escalators free of any defects.

Accident log

If an accident does occur, even the slightest cut or bruise, then record all the details in an accident logbook. Make sure your employees know to report all workplace accidents, no matter how minor.

Chemical labels

Clearly label chemicals and other substances to highlight proper use and potential hazards.

62. Raise morale and lower claims

Make a goal of building great morale, since a positive atmosphere can directly lower workers compensation claims. Build a business culture where teamwork and positive thinking prevail.

The construction industry is a potential breeding ground for workplace accidents. Steve manages his family's building firm and realised early on that on-the-job accidents can have an expensive and sometimes crippling effect on the profitability of his company. To counter this, Steve introduced a reward system for employees if a certain number of consecutive accident-free days were achieved. The staff really got behind the idea and they became very proud of their excellent safety record. Everyone worked hard to maintain an accident-free workplace, and nobody wanted to be the one to break the drought.

63. Promote health & fitness

Reduce health claims, injuries and sick leave by encouraging employees to maintain their health and fitness. Here are some great ideas to get your business healthy.

- Offer a reward for anyone who quits smoking.

- Provide a series of workshops for staff on topics such as nutrition, exercise and stress reduction.

- Encourage staff to enter a team in events such as fun runs, corporate sports events and other team activities.

- Provide secure areas to lock up bicycles for those staff that wish to ride to work.

- If your office is not on the ground floor, encourage staff to take the steps instead of the lift.

- Start an early morning walk, run or swim club with your staff, or an after-hours club for activities such as tennis or softball.

- Do away with junk food vending machines in your office.

■ Offer bonuses for employees who lose enough weight to place them in the normal range for age and height.

■ Publicise the savings in sick days and absenteeism.

Apart from the above savings, a healthy and closer team results in greater morale and higher productivity—and work is a much nicer place to be.

Staff training and development

Many businesses see training as an expense to be avoided. However, trained staff tend to be more efficient and productive, have fewer accidents and are usually happier and more motivated. Having well-trained and skilled staff is essential to the success of any business, but it is important to spend money in the right way. The following ideas will ensure you get the best return for your training dollar.

64. Get your suppliers to provide training

If your business has just invested thousands of dollars on machinery or equipment, get the supplier to provide free training sessions for the staff who will be using it. These employees can then go back and train the rest of the staff.

65. Benefit from free training

Utilise the free or low-cost services of relevant organisations to provide training for your staff in specific areas. Some organisations you may wish to contact include:

■ Emergency services—police, fire department, ambulance service

■ Red Cross

■ Neighbourhood Watch and Business Watch

■ Local government authority or shire council

■ Chamber of Commerce

- Relevant professional associations

- Surf Life Saving Australia and the Royal Life Saving Society Australia

Margaret, the owner of a drycleaners in a busy suburban shopping strip, organised a free training session on security issues for local businesses. Presentations were given for free by the local police and Neighbourhood Watch representatives. The fire brigade and emergency services representatives provided free fire awareness training for shopping centre staff and tenants. The two-hour session included a hands-on demonstration for all participants on the effective use of fire extinguishers and fire blankets.

You can even get your suppliers to provide free training. For example, if your business hires a security company to conduct regular patrols of your business premises, approach them to conduct a free security training session for your employees and provide a security audit of the premises. Similarly, if you use a security firm to collect your daily or weekly takings, have them conduct training for your staff on safe cash-handling procedures and armed hold-up procedures.

A client of mine operates a cleaning company and many of his employees are women. As the staff normally work either late at night or early in the morning they had some concerns about their own personal safety. I organised for another client who operates her own self-defence studio to provide a series of free 'Self-defence for women' workshops for the cleaning staff. This made them feel better prepared 'just in case' something was to happen, and the self-defence instructor picked up a number of new clients as some of the women chose to continue with the classes for a fee.

66. Don't waste money on the wrong training

Many businesses spend money on training that has little or no chance of making a difference to their bottom line. Does this sound familiar? If it does, then develop a list of skills that are critical to each position in your business and then put together a training plan to address the gaps in these skill areas.

For example, if you operate a women's fashion boutique you may identify the major skill areas for your sales staff as product knowledge, sales and merchandising.

Therefore, specific training would be required in the following areas.

- information about your latest range of clothes

- selecting the right style of clothes and colours for different customers

- building rapport with your customers

- determining customers' needs

- overcoming objections

- closing the sale

- cross-selling techniques

- arranging clothes for display purposes

Training in these skill areas will enable the sales staff to increase their customer service skills and selling ability, resulting in greater sales and higher sales volume.

Seminars where you are one of 2000 people sitting in a large conference arena are possibly not the best use of your training dollar. I know of very few people who have actually walked away from one of these extravaganzas and implemented positive changes in their business as a direct result of their attendance. Individual and small team mentoring programs are more effective, as they are designed to provide hands-on training tailored to the identified skill gaps of the individuals involved and specific to your business.

67. Use recapture agreements for training

Some employees work for businesses for a short period of time, receive a lot of training and then leave with that expertise to the benefit of another firm. This is becoming more common and is extremely costly to your business when they leave. For certain types of training, especially those that lead to some form of professional or occupational certification, it is a good idea to have employees sign a recapture agreement that calls for them to reimburse the employer on a pro rata basis for the cost of the training received if they leave prior to a specified time frame. These agreements will help your business protect your investment in your employees.

A marketing company hosted a yearly conference where all senior managers were flown in from around the world for a four-day event.

It wasn't just a junket but an intense planning session that not only reviewed the performance of the past twelve months but also set strategy for the coming year. After a couple of years of running these events, the company found that many managers resigned after returning from the conference. This resulted in a huge cost to the company, as they were receiving no return on the thousands of dollars spent for the managers to attend the conference. To counteract this huge loss, the company introduced a recapture agreement whereby any manager leaving within three months of the conference had to reimburse the company for the airfare and other expenses. Suffice to say, very few managers ever resigned again immediately after the conference. In fact, a shift resulted whereby resignations began to occur prior to the conference, thereby saving the company on travel and accommodation costs and also protecting their corporate strategies.

68. Bring the training to you

Instead of sending a number of employees to a specific training session, consider bringing a trainer to your location to conduct the training. If enough employees are involved, many training companies are willing to send someone to your business for a lot less than it would cost you to send the same number of employees to a training session. The session can be geared specifically to your business requirements and you will save on travel, time and other expenses.

69. Training without a budget

Trevor was a senior sales manager who wanted to upgrade the skills of his sales staff, but didn't have a training budget. He prepared a list of eight topics he wanted to cover and selected his top four sales managers. Each was assigned two of the subject areas and agreed to become the company expert on those issues. They gathered information from the library, Internet and other sources and put together a thirty-minute presentation on each subject. Every Wednesday for the next two months the group had pizzas for lunch along with a presentation on one of the assigned topics. The luncheons were a big hit as employees added to their skills and knowledge, all for the cost of a few pizzas. They also provided the added benefit of creating in-house experts that staff could refer to in the future if ever an issue was raised about any of the specific topics.

This clearly illustrates that with a little lateral thinking and the resources you already have at your disposal, you can develop a comprehensive and relevant training program for your employees—and it won't cost you a thing! All too often business owners and managers fail to give sufficient credit to the intelligence, abilities and capabilities of their number one resource—their staff. If they are given the appropriate guidance, support and opportunity, I guarantee that your employees will amaze you with what they can achieve and how much they can save you in the process.

70. Learn on-line

Computers and the Internet have resulted in numerous cost-saving advantages for businesses, and employee training is no exception. Many training companies now provide permanent on-line training programs that their customers can log on to at any time for on-line learning. You can now undertake short courses in just about anything—accounting, finance, marketing, human resource management, people management, conflict resolution, sales strategies, manufacturing, inventory control—the list is endless.

Your business can also use the Internet for your own internal training purposes.

For one marketing firm, the task of providing ongoing training and assessment for managers located in sales centres around the country could have proven a difficult and expensive exercise, were it not for the Internet. By logging on to a secure section of the company website at a given time, the managers could undertake relevant exams and assessment exercises from the comfort and convenience of their office. The employee had a given time period, usually two hours, in which to complete the necessary activities on-line. At the end of the time period the program would close down, preventing further information from being entered. The company's training and development manager would assess the work and then email the results back to each manager within twenty-four hours.

By effectively exploiting the Internet, this company saves tens of thousands of dollars each year on airfares, accommodation and time spent away from the office.

Staff remuneration

It's been mentioned a few times in this section and with good reason. When it comes to staff and their productivity, you get what you pay for. Underpaying employees will cost you in other ways, while overpaying unproductive staff is like flushing profits down the drain. The following tips will ensure you can create a profitable medium between rewarding your employees well and keeping your payroll costs under control.

71. How much should the boss be paid?

Small business owners often feel compelled to take large salaries and bonuses from their enterprise. And why not, you have worked extremely hard over a long period of time and it is your business after all. I'm certainly not against business owners paying themselves and even getting a Christmas bonus— we've all got to put food on the table. Problems arise however, when a business really cannot afford the extravagant amounts of money the owners and directors take for themselves. The news has been littered with examples of chief executives and directors receiving huge bonuses and redundancies while the business has suffered financially. OneTel and HIH are just two examples on an ever-lengthening list. In a growing business, cash is the glue that keeps everything together. There is no sense paying yourself a huge bonus one year only to have your business collapse in the ensuing months due to poor cash flow. Do adequately compensate yourself, but learn to know the difference between necessity and extravagance.

72. Wage increases should be earned

I am a firm believer that pay increases should be linked to an employee's performance and should not be considered an automatic benefit of their employment. Neither should increments be given based on how well an employee is liked or how long they have been with your business. This is throwing money away, as you're not getting anything in return. Your staff should be expected to perform at a high level and should be rewarded monetarily only when they meet or exceed these expectations. You must therefore clearly communicate to your employees the level of performance required of them and then be honest with them about their performance.

> *Gavin works for a law firm and in the past twelve months he has exceeded his budget by more than $100 000, yet he received the same pay increase that many of his colleagues received who underperformed. As a result, Gavin is looking for a job elsewhere and will be taking his energy, enthusiasm and considerable talent (along with an active client list) with him.*

Inappropriate pay increases are not only a waste of vital resources, they can destroy the morale of even your best and most loyal employees.

73. Don't short-change your employees

Your employees are your most important assets, and while the primary objective of your business is to make money, I don't recommend doing it at the expense of your employees. Holding employee wages down to boost your short-term profits is usually a big mistake. Your employees can effectively make or break your business so what you save in wages, you will probably lose twofold in high staff turnover, increased recruitment costs, and low staff morale resulting in poor service and loss of business.

> *In my first year of university, I took a job working two nights a week as a doorman for a small one-screen suburban cinema. After my first week I realised that I was working for a real scrooge. June, who owned and managed the cinema, was well known for paying very low wages and being an extremely strict employer. Unfortunately for June, she didn't realise that the savings she was making by paying her staff a paltry wage, she was actually losing threefold in other ways. I soon discovered that it was common practice for staff to let in their friends and family to see a movie for free. As June never did a stocktake, the guy running the kiosk would always hand out free ice-creams and chocolates to the other staff. The projectionist was so demotivated that he regularly fell asleep on the job and many a*

time I had to run upstairs and wake him up as the film reel had finished and he hadn't switched over the projectors. This resulted in the cinema getting a reputation for poor quality and customers started to drive fifteen minutes further to another cinema in a neighbouring suburb.

As the old saying goes, you get what you pay for. June's business suffered tremendously because her staff had little respect for an employer who would pay them so badly.

74. Don't pay your staff as often

Many businesses are reducing their payroll costs by paying rank and file staff fortnightly instead of weekly. Some are taking it a step further by paying their management staff monthly. This has significant savings for your business, as payroll is processed less frequently. Savings accrue from the time taken to calculate, write and distribute payments, plus lower monthly bank charges. Any significant changes in payroll procedure will be met with some resistance by employees, so smart management will sell the idea to them months in advance.

Michael owns a fashion and accessories store and has a team of eight staff. In order to reduce his payroll costs, Michael changed from weekly to fortnightly pays and negotiated with his manager to place her on a monthly payroll cycle. As many of his staff were used to being paid weekly, Michael gave six weeks notice that pays would be changing to the new system, so that his employees could plan well ahead. He also held an information session on how to manage the change from living on a weekly to a fortnightly pay. Thanks to this one simple change, his projected administration savings were around $8000 over a twelve-month period.

75. Running your business is kids' stuff

One of the quickest ways to reduce your payroll costs while maintaining the same level of staffing is to employ teenagers. Most award structures align an employee's wage with their age and their experience. By employing younger and less experienced workers you could be saving a couple of dollars an hour for each person you employ, compared to what you would have to pay for someone over the age of 21 who has much more experience.

> *Teenagers account for a high proportion of staff working at fast food chains like McDonald's and Pizza Hut. And have you noticed cinema staff? You'll struggle to find anyone over the age of 20, but the service is bright, cheery and professional. Some of the best telemarketers I have ever known were only 17 or 18 years of age.*

There are probably many positions in your organisation that could be competently handled by teenagers or young adults. So next time a position becomes vacant, see how you could engage some youthful exuberance into your business and save money at the same time. Now before any activists start jumping up and down and claiming that I am promoting child slave labour, I'm not. As long as you pay your employees in accordance with the standards set by the government, there should be no cause for concern. Many young people need to work just as much as adults do, and let's face it, we probably all know at least one or two successful entrepreneurs who started on their road to corporate dominance by flipping burgers on a weekend.

76. Penalty rates

If your business operates on weekends, evenings and public holidays, no doubt you have to pay penalty rates for all staff on duty. Penalty rates can literally double your payroll bill and there is no escaping them, as in most cases the requirement to pay these higher rates is a matter of law. There are, however, a number of things you can do to reduce the impact penalty rates will have on your payroll budget.

- Check your staffing levels to ensure you don't have too many people standing around doing nothing and getting paid handsomely for it.

- Use junior staff during these periods. Paying time and a half to a 17-year-old may be the same as or lower than what you pay your more senior employees.

- Alternatively, use salaried rather than casual staff so you do not have to pay them penalty rates.

- For sales positions, employ your best staff in the hope of maximising sales during this period.

- Provide an added incentive to staff if they achieve a certain sales volume.

- Hold special promotions during these times to try and generate extra sales.

- Determine whether you really need to open and if you do, then do you need to stay open for as long as you do. Simply opening or closing one hour earlier could save you thousands of dollars in wages over the course of a year, and have no negative impact on your business.

- Incorporate a surcharge into your prices to help cover the increase in staff wages.

77. Overtime

Overtime can also add a considerable amount of money to your payroll. Where possible, it should be completely avoided, as the costs far outweigh the benefits. So is overtime a problem for your business? If it is, maybe these ideas will help you keep it under control.

- Go back through your wages reports and determine the exact extent of your overtime payments and reasons given as to why overtime was worked.

- Instead of getting existing staff to work overtime, hire extra part-time or casual workers to fill in the gaps.

- Look for ways to make your staff more productive so they complete all the necessary tasks in the time that they have been allocated.

- Negotiate with staff to take time in lieu as an alternative to paid overtime.

- If the overtime is for a one-off event, get your employees to work for free—allow them to dress casually and throw on a few pizzas or coffee and donuts.

- Get organised. Much of the overtime paid by small businesses comes from a lack of organisation and planning.

- Sometimes, no matter how well organised you are, something crops up out of nowhere. In these instances it may be a case of all hands on deck, yourself included.

- Overtime should always be approved beforehand.

78. Use non-cash rewards to save costs

If there are two things I've learned in all my years in business they are firstly, it's a fact that everyone wants to be appreciated and secondly, money isn't necessarily the most effective way of showing that appreciation. Watch productivity surge when you creatively motivate and energise your staff with personalised low-cost rewards.

- Give praise in front of the rest of the team.

- Honour outstanding performances of the month for sales, customer service and production.

- Have a surprise party when milestones or records are achieved.

- Remember staff birthdays, anniversaries and other important occasions and celebrate them.

- Write productive staff a thank you note and post it to their home.

- Take a staff member to lunch as a way of saying thanks or well done.

- Create a Wall of Fame containing memos, notes and awards received by all staff for jobs well done.

The list could go on forever. A quick trip to any bookstore will ensure you have enough low-cost ideas to last you a lifetime.

79. Give staff a share of the profits

If you really want your employees to work hard at saving costs, increasing productivity and generating greater revenue and profits, give them a reason—give them a share of the profits.

A friend told me how a few years ago his retail company ran a competition for all the different stores in an effort to reduce overheads and increase profits. Each individual store was set a target to increase sales and profits. If this target was achieved, a share of the profits would be divided among all employees of that store. The competition was run over three months and not surprisingly the company owners noticed a marked decrease in expenditure, the implementation of a number of innovative cost-saving measures and a subsequent increase in profits. What was surprising was that once the competition finished and things went back to normal, expenditure began to increase once again and many of the initiatives developed to save costs were no longer carried out.

So give your staff a piece of the action. Set a target, tell them what it is and then let them go for it, and whenever they begin to question why they are recycling that piece of paper or turning the lights off they'll remember how these actions are putting money in their pockets.

80. Compensating sales staff

Compensating salespeople in a manner that rewards them appropriately and that truly provides an incentive to stretch to higher levels of performance is sometimes a difficult balancing act. Some business owners are reluctant to structure sales compensation plans that could allow their sales reps to earn significant incomes. On numerous occasions my top salespeople have earned more than I have in a month. But they worked damn hard to get it and as a result of their efforts I was invariably meeting my targets as well. To me, it was money well spent.

A sales company I know very well sets a minimum target for their salespeople of ten sales per week before any commission is paid. If a consultant works their tail off and still only manages nine sales, the company does not reward them with any bonus. The reasoning behind this strategy is simple. The bare minimum expectation the company has is that sales staff must make ten sales to receive any further rewards. Paying commission to someone who makes fewer than ten sales is rewarding them for underachievement.

You need to set your compensation plan so that it rewards staff for achieving beyond the minimum standard expected. If you reward salespeople for underachieving, you are flushing money down the drain.

81. Save costs with reduced absenteeism

Absenteeism, valid or otherwise, can cost your business thousands of dollars in lost productivity and overtime payments. In many cases, it is difficult to determine whether the absent employee is telling the truth or just taking advantage of the system to have some paid time off. Here are five strategies that you can implement immediately to help reduce absenteeism.

Keep records of absenteeism

It is imperative that you know how often your employees have been absent and the reason for it. Geoff ran a busy call centre for a timeshare company and he employed 40 part-time consultants. With so many staff, it was easy to lose track of how many days each staff had been absent due to illness or otherwise. As all staff were paid for a set amount of holiday and sick pay, it was important that accurate records were kept. Before implementing a recording system Geoff estimated that he had overpaid staff about $500 worth of wages for holiday and sick leave they were not entitled to.

Address attendance in appraisals

Make work attendance a formal and integral part of your employees' performance appraisals. By doing so you are sending out a clear message that regular absenteeism is unacceptable and may result in a loss of job or a loss of pay. Employees will soon get the idea that you have zero tolerance for deceptive absenteeism.

Check references for attendance

Do you check a new employee's attendance record in their previous positions before you employ them? A check of their references is a bright way of discovering those people who habitually take time off work. Remember, prevention is better than cure.

Reward employees for excellent attendance

Many small businesses are now paying a cash bonus to employees who do not miss a single day of work during a twelve-month period. Or instead of cash, you could give them a couple of extra days paid holiday.

Publicise excellent attendance records

Have a regular segment in your company newsletter or post a bulletin on the staff noticeboard listing excellent attendance records.

82. Underperforming staff can cost you money

It seems that most businesses have at least one employee that is underperforming or may be causing some sort of internal disruption. Employee problems have a direct impact on your bottom line if they are not dealt with expediently. Non-performing staff are also a drain on your resources. If they are not meeting their targets or undertaking their duties in an appropriate way, they are no doubt costing you money.

Dan was a headstrong salesman who had a real problem focusing on the job at hand. A real ladies' man, he would spend most of his time chatting up the female members of staff or trying to attract attention to himself by cracking jokes and disturbing the rest of the sales team. While he was a likeable bloke and did have the ability to be a decent salesman, Dan's behaviour was having a negative impact on the team and his own results were slipping dramatically. His manager had discussed his performance with him on a number of occasions but with very little improvement. One day, Dan's boss pulled him aside and gave him a written warning regarding his behaviour in the sales office and recent lack of poor sales. Unable to deal with this affront to his ego, Dan stormed out of the office never to be seen again. The relief in the sales room was immediate and the team posted their highest day of sales for the past three months.

It is your responsibility as a small business owner to make the tough decision and deal with underperforming or problem employees straight away. If left to fester, they end up affecting those staff around them and disrupting team harmony and productivity.

83. Avoiding costly staff terminations

The firing of an employee can be an unpleasant task for a manager or business owner. In today's market, termination can no longer be a matter of managerial whim. You must do your homework and ensure your actions satisfy the relevant legislative requirements (in Australia, the *Workplace Relations Act 1996*). It is no longer acceptable to dismiss someone with only the requisite period of notice. You must make sure that the employee is:

■ given a valid reason for the dismissal (preferably in writing)

■ given a chance to respond to allegations

■ warned in writing on a previous occasion about their conduct

■ given another opportunity to meet stated performance standards.

When an employee's termination is deemed to be unfair, the courts may order reinstatement and payment of lost wages, and possibly other compensation too. Add to this court costs and legal fees, and an unfair dismissal case can be a costly exercise for your business.

3

STATIONERY AND OFFICE SUPPLIES

The problem with most small businesses is that they are only interested in cost-saving ideas that will save them thousands. The reality, however, is that small reductions across a multitude of areas can amount to huge savings. One area where this applies most is in the purchase and use of stationery and office supplies. The following suggestions will help you get more sense from your dollars.

Chapter 3

Stationery and office supplies

This chapter covers:

84. When quality doesn't count

What lies in a fridge often says a lot about that family. The same can be said for any business; however, in this case we can swap the fridge for the stationery cabinet. I just love walking into a business and making a beeline for the bulging cupboard that is often overflowing with enough office supplies to give WC Penfolds a run for their money. And it's not just the number of items that amazes me—it's also the quality. Why some business people choose to buy the Rolls Royce version of office supplies I'll never understand.

The following common office stationery items are notorious money wasters in most businesses.

Calculators

Do you or your employees really need that $120 super model calculator or can you get by with the $15 version? In my experience, most small businesses only require a calculator for simple calculations such as addition, subtraction and working out percentages.

Staplers

Why spend $70 (yes, $70) for a stapler when you can get a cheaper model that does the same job for less than $10. I bought my trusty little stapler two years ago for $5 and it's still going strong despite a hefty workout every day.

Hole punchers

Can you believe you can also pay up to $70 for a hole puncher? Let's get serious, most offices can manage with a $6 one—they both put holes in paper.

Liquid paper

Liquid paper is my pet hate. Why is it necessary in this day and age of computer technology? Your staff shouldn't be using it for documents being sent to your customers, as it looks unprofessional. It's not required for internal documents or messages and it is certainly a big no-no when doing your accounts. If you use it for any handwritten work, simply cross out the mistake and write the correct information next to it. White-out liquid paper from your shopping list today!

Post-it® notes

Post-it® notes are probably the greatest invention in office stationery but the biggest money waster. These little yellow (now almost any colour) notes with the self-adhesive back can cost your business. Either write directly on the main piece of paper or use a piece of scrap paper and staple it to the top right-hand corner.

Business card holders

The small plastic box that is home to all the business cards you acquire but probably never refer to, and which normally hides in your desk drawer, can cost you upwards of $25. Head for the $2 shop and pick up a bargain that can hold 400 business cards.

I could go on forever but I think you get the message. There are two important points here. The first is that the small business owner needs to determine the difference between what is practical and functional, and what is extravagance. And the difference could mean huge savings for your business. The second consideration is how you control the purchasing of office supplies. Does your administration person have a free hand to purchase what they want, or have you made it clear as to what is acceptable? A good tip is to implement some form of control. This is not over-management but sound management.

85. Put it away

In many offices, pilferage of stationery items such as pens, paper, staplers and calculators can really take its toll. Take a leaf out of every good secretary's book. Clear the top of your desk at the end of each day. Put your stationery items in your desk drawer and lock it up if possible. I once asked a secretary why she and her colleagues did this, and the reply was 'to stop stuff getting pinched, of course'. And when your stationery cupboard is bare, before you go shopping for more get all your staff (yourself included) to dig through their desks, briefcases, cabinets and stationery holders for extra supplies. You'll be amazed at how much you will find—a long-lost stapler or calculator and at least two dozen pens and pencils.

86. Little things do add up

This may sound pedantic and stingy to some, but how many of you recycle your rubber bands, paper clips, pins, manila folders, report binders and cover sheets? What if I told you that I saved my business over $200 in a year just on these things alone? Success is in the detail.

87.   Reuse paper and save big

Paper for printing and copying can be a huge cost for your business. Paper is also bulky, so large amounts of it can also take up a lot of storage space. However, there are plenty of things you can do to dramatically reduce the costs and save your business.

Use both sides

Always try to use both sides of a sheet of paper for printing, copying, writing and doodling.

Junk mail is good

Don't immediately throw away the junk mail as it comes in. You can print on the blank side of the letters, notices and A4 flyers that find their way into your letterbox.

Turn old into new

Clear out all those old files and reuse the paper. Cut up less sensitive documents into small notepad squares or shred them. Print or photocopy onto the blank side of other paper.

Faxes/printing/photocopying

Use reused paper for receiving faxes, printing internal documents and photocopying. Manual feeding will avoid any jamming of the paper in the equipment. Make sure the information on the original document is not of a sensitive nature.

Efficient copying

Use the size reduction function on the photocopier to copy two pages onto one, and place a notice on the copier explaining how to properly load printers and copiers so the correct side of the paper will be used (see also Chapter 4).

I have constantly used all of these ideas with great success. When I was managing a sales centre in Brisbane, we did not spend a single cent on purchasing paper over a period of 16 months. I calculated that this saved my company over $800 on printing and copying paper. Not only is recycling great for the earth's environment, it's also terrific for your business's environment.

88. Save with proper storage

If paper that you intend to reuse is stored properly, you will have no trouble with it jamming up fax machines, printers or photocopiers. A good idea is to put all reusable paper in the cardboard box that the original A4 paper came in. This will keep everything flat and in good order, ready for use. And no more jams, as long as you remove all the staples.

89. Size does matter ... and it saves you money

Can you remember back to your early school days and the writing pads and notebooks you were given? Thick, rough paper crisscrossed with lines about one inch apart, wide enough to cater for your large, clumsy but enthusiastic handwriting. As you got older the paper got better and the lines grew closer together, because our educators understood that with age came smaller, neater and more controlled writing and more writing could fit on one page. So take some guidance from them—if you do purchase lined paper, buy the narrow lined pads. When printing internal memos or draft reports, use a smaller font size and narrower margins. You'll fit more on one page and use less paper. Size does matter and small is good.

90. Clean disks

Computer disks are no different from filing cabinets. After a while they get full of stuff that nobody needs or wants or knows what to do with. Instead of filing the disks away or throwing them out, why not reuse them. Regularly go through your disks and delete any files that are no longer required. This will free up more space and in some cases provide you with empty disks to use. One day my secretary found forty-five old disks sitting in a cupboard, which she was about to throw out when I volunteered to take them off her hands. I went through each one and deleted basically everything, then ran the disks through the virus scan and they were ready for reuse. This little exercise took ten minutes and saved me around $40.

91. Save on disks

Speaking of computer disks, try to save as much information on disks rather than in hard copy paper format. If your computer doesn't have it then

I recommend you install Winzip—this neat little function reduces the size of a document and enables you to save large pieces of information into smaller files. It will not only save you paper and photocopying costs, but will definitely reduce the number of filing cabinets you require.

92. Inter-office correspondence

Don't waste your good quality company envelopes on sending internal correspondence between departments or offices. Reusing inter-office envelopes cuts waste of this stationery item. These C4 size envelopes are used to send correspondence from one office to another. Purchase them from any stationery store or recycle a used C4 envelope. Make a cover sheet on your computer with about thirty lines down the page and divided into two columns. In the left column put the header 'From' and the right column 'To'. Stick this to the front of the envelope, which can then be recycled. If the information you are sending is not confidential, you can do away with the envelope altogether and staple a piece of scrap paper to the top right-hand corner with the name of the recipient.

93. A window of savings

If you are mailing a lot of correspondence, consider buying some window-faced envelopes, with the see-through window at the front through which you can see the address of the recipient. These envelopes will save you time and money in the following ways.

■ You don't have to print or buy address labels for the envelopes.

■ You don't have to spend time sticking labels onto envelopes.

■ There is no double printing of the address because it already appears on the letter and this can be seen through the window.

■ You will reduce packaging time.

Mary manages a very successful small direct mail business from her home. She sends out over 1000 direct mail pieces every week. When she first started her business, it was a case of handwriting the delivery address details on the front of each envelope and her address on the back. As her business grew, she changed to window envelopes *and has never looked back. This small idea has saved her over $200 per week (those address labels are really expensive) and freed up a further three hours, which she uses on other revenue-generating activities.*

94. Tie down savings

Many businesses have pens lying around the reception area for people to complete order forms or write down details. Have you noticed how your pens are always disappearing? It might seem trivial but I know of a small business owner who used to go through one box of blue pens every week through loss and pilferage. That equates to about $250 per year on pens! So go ahead and tie those pens to the front counter or clipboard. If putting pens on chains is good enough for banks, insurance companies and other big businesses, it is certainly good enough for you. And remind staff to return the bundle of pens that collect at home after emptying their pockets or bags at the end of the day.

95. Who are those company notepads for again?

Many businesses spend money printing message pads with their company logo and contact details to give away to their customers and prospects. If your business has these notepads, then why are you and your staff keeping them for internal use? I am amazed at the number of businesses where I see the administration staff scribbling on these expensive notepads that should be sitting on a customer's desk reminding them of why they do business with you, or better still, sitting on the desk of a potential customer screaming, 'Come and do business with us'. Get them out of your office and into the offices of customers and potential customers, and stop wasting money.

96. Latch on to freebies

Grand openings, trade shows, festivals, conferences and seminars often give away pens, rulers, notebooks and the like. Now I am not suggesting that you take time away from your busy schedule just to pick up a free pen or two, but if you are already attending these events then make the most of the opportunities as they present themselves.

In the three years that I managed a twenty-person call centre, I didn't buy a single pen. All my pens were kindly 'donated' by potential and existing suppliers, numerous industry trade shows and conferences I attended and also courtesy of the many five-star hotels I stayed in. I worked out that I must have saved over $500 in pens in three years. I remember at one conference when the event was officially closed, I walked around and started collecting all the pens and notepads left behind by the delegates. A couple of attendees (with whom I have since become good friends) asked me what I was doing. I told them of the cost-saving benefits and it has now become a ritual at all events we attend. The best part is when the three of us are at the same event: it's a scramble at the end to see who can collect the most items!

97. Make your own

Consider adapting to stationery the do-it-yourself idea advocated in Chapter 1. A secretary I used to work with loved to drink Coca-Cola, and so she cut off the tops of Coke cans, cut some of them in half and turned them into her desktop stationery organiser. She told me she preferred this to a normal desk organiser because it was something personal. Not all of us are as creative, so do what I do and use one of the many free mugs you are given at trade fares, conferences, product openings and by your suppliers. They make excellent pen holders. Also, instead of throwing away envelopes when you open your mail, use the back of them for making notes.

Have a look around your business. What else can you apply a do-it-yourself (or make-it-yourself) strategy to?

98. A pin-up idea to save money

Many offices have noticeboards for staff to use, and the items that go on these boards are often more personal than work-related. Noticeboards can be pretty expensive, especially if you have to buy a few of them. The following idea saved me over $1000 when I set up a sales office in the Philippines. Instead of buying cork noticeboards, I purchased 50 ft of 2 ft x 8 ft sheets of foam and a few rolls of double-sided poster tape, and stuck the foam on the wall. To make it more presentable, I then covered the foam with some brightly coloured old bed sheets. Once I had stuck all the notices, memos and other information on the board, it looked fantastic. Better still, I only spent around $100 instead of the quoted $1200 to purchase noticeboards. A cheaper alternative is to just stick sheets of coloured card on the wall. This provides a colourful background on which to post those memos, notes and reminders.

CHAPTER

4

PHOTOCOPYING AND PRINTING

Even before computers and the Internet were commonplace, many successful small business operators were moving towards a paperless society and saving themselves a bundle at the same time. The novel ideas in this chapter are guaranteed to not only reduce your printing costs but help save the planet as well.

Chapter 4

Photocopying and Printing

This chapter covers:

99. Photocopying your savings

Rent, buy or get the best price! Check your photocopying contract or agreement to make sure you are getting the best deal—and if you're not, renegotiate or go elsewhere. I worked in an office building where the photocopier machine and paper were provided and all we paid was 20c per copy. The suppliers took care of the servicing and everything else. While our photocopying was not in huge quantities—or so we thought—we found a copy centre directly adjacent to our office which could do the same job for 7c per copy. I monitored our photocopying costs over the next month and calculated that we had saved $50 in general copying costs. That equates to $600 a year!

And while we are on the subject, here are a few other bright ideas to help reduce your photocopying costs even further.

■ Minimise the number of misprints and paper jams by posting a diagram above the photocopier explaining how to load special paper such as letterhead so it will print correctly.

■ Appoint a 'keeper of the photocopier', whose role is to train all staff, old and new, on the proper use of the photocopier and the many features it has, such as manual feed, double-sided printing, size reduction, sorting, collating and stapling. Or, have the supplier come around and give staff an informal training session, then pick someone who can train new employees.

■ Use the size reduction feature to copy two pages onto one piece of paper. This simple idea will literally cut your photocopying costs in half.

100. Do you really need a copy?

Learn to determine whether you need to take a copy of something or not. Often we photocopy things out of habit, only to have that piece of paper (along with hundreds of others) sit in a filing cabinet taking up valuable space, never to be read again.

I once worked in a business that I am sure had shares in Fuji Xerox! In their desire to keep everyone informed about everything going on in the organisation they photocopied and distributed a personal copy of all relevant memos, notices and reports to every staff member. I had to get a bigger in-tray because the flood of paper was so great. If you want to keep people updated but don't want to waste time and money on making so many copies, consider the following.

Centralised records section

Devise a system whereby coded files are developed for each particular subject and kept in a central filing system. Only one copy is needed and only one filing cabinet as well.

Circulation list

Make one copy and attach a circulation list to the top right-hand corner. This should list the names of all people required to read the document. If you work in a larger organisation, the circulation list may be the names of all the relevant departments. When one department has read the document, they sign next to their name and pass it on to the next on the list.

Public copies

Take a few copies and post them around your business where staff are likely to see them—on staff noticeboards, above tea and coffee facilities, near the photocopier and even in the toilets on the back of cubicle doors and above handbasins—I guarantee no one will miss this notice!

The reduction in the number of copies you require has a savings flow-on effect into other areas of your business. Firstly, you save on photocopying, paper and toner charges. At the same time you reduce the amount of staff time used to make the copies, plus the number of files, manila folders, filing cabinets and bookshelves required to store them in. With less storage facilities, you may also be able to reduce the size of your office, saving you on office rental charges. It just goes to show, one small cost reduction idea can be the catalyst for much greater savings.

101. Refill your printer cartridges

Since almost all printer cartridges are refillable, either purchase the refill ink kits or have the cartridge refilled by one of the many companies that recycle toner cartridges. This can literally save you thousands of dollars a year.

It was my third day on the job as senior sales manager for an international marketing firm, and my officer manager realised we needed a new toner cartridge. She said she would go down to one of *the major stationery suppliers nearby and get a new one for $150. Over my dead body! A quick scan of the local business paper put out by the chamber of commerce and we found a company that recycles the cartridges for only $70 a pop. At a saving of $80 per cartridge we stood to save around $1000 a year based on projected usage.*

Speak to your toner supplier about alternatives to the major name brands. By doing this I saved around $10 extra buying a generic brand that lasted just as long and provided excellent print quality. Here are two more tips to save on toner cartridges.

- When the print quality from your printer begins to fade then remove the cartridge and shake it vigorously to redistribute the remaining toner. This can be done several times to prolong the life of the cartridge.

- Use cartridges that are almost empty to print out draft documents or documents for internal use.

102. Proofreading

The advent of the computer has made many of us lazy and this has resulted in much loss and wastage for many businesses. Spelling or grammatical faux pas can cost your business big time. Before printing any document ensure you proofread it and run the spell and grammar check over it.

It was early 1991 and I was undertaking postgraduate studies in marketing. One subject of particular interest was direct marketing. Keen to put my new skills to use, I soon had the opportunity to develop a direct mail promotion for the company I was working for at the time. I enthusiastically sent out a direct mail letter to 500 customers and eagerly waited for the phones to ring. Unfortunately, the first call I took brought me back to reality with a sickening thump, as I was politely informed by an observant client that I had made three critical spelling errors. It was extremely embarrassing and a dent to my pride and the image of my company. I quickly redrafted another letter and sent it to every one of the 500 customers. It announced the first person that had called regarding the spelling mistake was the winner of a fabulous gift pack of company products and the whole affair was a deliberate ploy to see how many people *had actually read our mailing piece. The letter went on to further describe the product we were originally trying to promote. Some quick thinking managed to save our credibility, but the blunder cost an extra $1000 in postage, stationery, printing, time and crisis management.*

Take it from me, the extra minute or two it takes to check spelling and grammar, review the print preview, refer to a dictionary or even get a colleague to proof your work is a small price to pay in comparison to the potential loss and embarrassment both you and your business could suffer. Asking a colleague to proof a document may help in other ways too—a fresh pair of eyes can improve as well as correct.

103. Reformat to save

Have a long, hard look at all the forms and documents you use in your business. By simply reducing their size or format, you can save a lot of money.

Joe runs his own lawnmowing service and markets his business around the neighbourhood by placing flyers in residents' letterboxes. He came up with the idea of reformatting his flyer so he could fit two onto one A4 page. This effectively cut paper and copying costs in half, saving him around $300 a year. In another example, Jenny reformatted her customer order form so it appeared on the bottom portion of her cover letter, saving her direct mail business over $750 a year.

104. Your letters can save you money

Tremendous savings can be made from the endless pieces of correspondence that come out of your business. The simple act of posting a letter certainly won't send you bankrupt, but you can save money in two easy ways. Firstly, if you are sending out a letter that is two pages in length, then print the second page on the reverse side of the letterhead. Not only does this save you money on paper, it may also reduce your postage costs and you don't have the hassle of trying to fold two pages. Secondly, I shudder every time I receive a two-page letter from a business, only to find that the second separate page contains just one short sentence and the author's salutation. What a waste! Why not try to fit your letter on the one page by being succinct in what you say and using smaller font sizes. Or, make full use of the second page. Include more relevant information in the main body of the letter or add something interesting as a postscript.

105. Control your urge to print

For many of us, hitting the print command on our computer is a reflex action. In most cases though, I would question whether we actually need a hard (printed) copy of that information. Here are some ways to help you control your printing next time you're on the computer.

- Review draft documents on the computer rather than printing them out. This takes a little getting used to as many of us are accustomed to reading a hard copy but it will save you time and money.

- Read documents on the computer and only print them if you really need to.

- Store documents on the computer hard drive or on a floppy disk.

- Check the type of paper in the printer before use. This avoids printing a draft document on company letterhead. If your printer has more than one tray, use one for clear paper and the other for letterhead, and clearly label them.

- Most printers enable you to set the quality or the density of the print much like a photocopier does. Set it to an economy grade for all your internal printing. It is a small step but one which will save you over the long run.

- Consider purchasing a duplex printer that prints both sides of a page at once. If you can't afford this, be sure to manually print on both sides of the paper.

- There is also computer software available that enables you to print two pages on the one sheet, similar to the function on a photocopier. This is great, especially if you print a lot of lengthy documents.

- Set narrow margins (0.5 inch) on your page set up, and use single spacing and smaller font sizes and types.

106. Tell your printer you are saving costs

If you use them, then let your graphic artist, printer and advertising agency know that you want to save costs but still require a quality product. They're the experts, so force them to make the cost-conscious choices necessary to save you money. This includes decisions on factors such as the number of ink colours to be used, paper weight and quality, cover pages, binding requirements, the size of the print run and the extent of photos, graphics and illustrations used.

Susan managed a major state-wide public relations campaign promoting healthy lifestyles. She called for tenders to design and print all the promotional material and stationery. Once the best tender was selected, they were asked to see how they could provide the same design as originally tendered but for $10 000 less. It was a big call but the designer had a few tricks up their sleeve and managed to reduce the quote by just over $11 000. The result was still a quality product.

107. Save on colour

Colour can certainly add life to your promotional material and business stationery. However, it can also add considerable cost. The following are ways to give your business a colourful look without the colourful price tag.

One-colour printing without black

The single colour used in one-colour printing does not have to be black. Using an alternative such as blue or brown in different shades can give the impact of colour without the cost.

Effective two-colour printing with black

If chosen correctly, you can use black and one colour and still create some serious impact. The business logo for my company, The Bright Ideas Manager, uses black and bright yellow on white paper. This simple colour combination creates a dramatic effect and in doing so saves me a bundle on paper and printing costs.

A four-colour look with two colours

Is printing in four-colour really necessary? Did you know that using two-colour print often allows you to use a number of different shades of the main colour?

The end result is a full colour look for a two-colour price. Alternatively, use two colours rather than black and one colour. In my opinion, four-colour printing is overkill for many small to medium businesses.

Paper

Can you use brightly coloured paper to achieve a noticeable effect? I have received letters and promotional material from many small businesses using black print on coloured paper—and they looked great.

And if you are on a really tight budget, then consider this bright idea. Most businesses choose to use coloured paper for many of their promotional flyers and notices because it creates impact and makes their message stand out from the clutter. You can achieve a similar impact by using normal white paper with graphics. Coloured paper is about three times more expensive than white paper so incorporating some eye-catching graphics can help your work get noticed. Most computers have a 'clip art' package that gives you a range of graphics.

108. Save on your corporate identity

Having the right business stationery is a crucial decision all business operators need to make. Your letterhead, business cards and brochures go a long way towards defining your position in the marketplace and creating an easily identifiable image. However, a powerful and effective corporate image doesn't have to cost you a bomb.

Paper quality

Think long and hard about the quality of paper stock that you use for letterhead. Do you really require super glossy or heavy grained paper? Does it suit the image your business is trying to portray? Can you reduce the quality slightly? Generally you will find that it makes little noticeable difference to the quality, but a worthwhile saving to your bottom line.

When your paper quality is too good

Glossy, shiny paper stock can give your stationery a super professional or super sexy look—depending upon which image you're going for. However, this can be too much of a good thing. I once spent a morning in an office supplies store trying to find a pen that could write on the 'With compliments' slips and customer referral cards provided by a client for whom I was running a marketing promotion. The client wanted to have a five-star look, which they achieved, but it came at a price. We literally could not find a single pen that would write on the slips and cards, so they were wasted. Even worse, the promotion certainly lost business because the customer couldn't write on the referral cards.

'With compliments' slips

Are these really necessary for your business? I'm amazed when I receive information in the mail and a 'With comp' slip is attached with nothing written on it. This slip of paper can be a powerful sales and marketing tool if used properly—for instance, including a personal handwritten message referring to your previous telephone conversation. 'With compliments' slips are just a huge waste of money unless you use them properly. So do so, and let them help you make money rather than waste it.

Envelopes

My friend Bill has two sets of envelopes. The first set are his good quality envelopes complete with company name and logo and a few bits of other information. Bill uses these for all his sales and marketing activities, when he wants to make an impression. The second set is for sending out invoices, receipts and other general correspondence. Bill's motto is to 'spend money on money-making activities—anything else, keep it simple'. Wise words, Bill.

Company logo

Believe it or not, I know of many small businesses that print faxes onto their company letterhead. Don't waste your good (and possibly expensive) business stationery for faxes—it's only going to come out in black and white at the other end. Instead, scan your company's logo into your computer and use this for preparing faxed messages and emails.

Tax invoices

I received a tax invoice the other day that closely resembled a work of art. It is now lying at the bottom of a drawer with all my other receipts and probably won't see the light of day until I sit down to do my books at the end of the next tax period. Don't waste your coloured letterhead on tax invoices and receipts. I really don't care what your invoices look like—I'm only interested in the cost—as long as they have all the relevant information, and I'm sure the same goes for most other people.

Print your own

You can save your business a great deal of money by printing your own letterhead, invoices and 'With compliments' slips using your office printer. By using black copy on white or lightly coloured paper you can achieve professional-looking corporate identity for next to nothing. Karim prints all his own stationery using his laser printer. The customers of his lawnmowing business don't expect him to have glossy, full-colour stationery, and neither does he.

109. Print in bulk

Printing in bulk can save your business a great deal. As mentioned in Chapter 1, one of my first products was a successful self-published manual that was sold via direct mail. Initially, I could only afford to have twenty copies printed at a time. As my business and the demand for the publication grew, I was able to have much larger numbers printed. Every time I increased the size of the print run, the cost of printing became less. I currently have one hundred copies printed at a time and the difference in cost is just on $1 per copy. At the current rate of sales for that one publication alone, I stand to save over $2000 in printing costs this year.

110. Keep it simple and save on printing

Printing doesn't have to be a costly exercise. The printing requirements of many small businesses are fairly basic in nature and it is this simplicity that can afford you big savings.

Add-ons

Next time you want some simple, low-cost, single-sided promotional flyers printed, negotiate with your printer to do them at the end of someone else's print run. You might not get a choice in the colour of ink or paper but it doesn't really matter as the costs will be greatly reduced, or you may not be charged at all. All the printer has to do is change the plate containing your artwork and away they print.

'On the floor' stock

You can save up to 30 per cent on the paper costs of your next printing job by using standard paper stock that your printer already has in their inventory.

If your printer has to order in special paper, your costs will increase, so ask them to quote your next print job using paper that they already have on hand. Even better, ask if they have any paper that has been sitting around the storeroom floor for more than six months. If they have then there is a good chance that no one wants to use it, so it is costing the printer to have it taking up space. Negotiate to use that paper for the same price you were going to pay for normal paper.

Gang print

Tell your printer to coordinate your print job with that of another business and do them both at the same time. Part of the cost of printing involves preparing the press and the clean-up afterwards. By doing all your printing at the same time, you pay only once for the preparation and clean-up. For example, your printer may already have another job using blue ink, so they could print that one and your job at the same time. Two jobs, one colour, less work for the printer and a reduced price for you.

III. Promotion shell

Here's a method of saving you heaps on printing promotional pieces. Prepare and print a standard 'promotional shell'. This can consist of your business name and logo, contact details and maybe a couple of photos or graphics. The rest of the page is left blank. You simply prepare information of your next promotion on your PC and print or photocopy them onto the shell. I have seen this strategy used successfully by hotels, resorts, garden centres, stationery suppliers, computer stores, booksellers and even churches. Along with saving you money, this strategy will help your business to develop a consistent image within the marketplace.

II2. Print en masse

A major budgetary headache for many small businesses is the printing costs of brochures, flyers, sales material, letterhead, business cards and the like. Like budget savers mentioned in previous chapters, one way to bring this cost into check is to coordinate your printing needs with those of other small businesses. The commitment of a small army of small businesses to one exclusive printer can enable you to command a significant discount for your printing requirements.

And it's really simple to do. Grab a pen right now and list the names of the ten businesses nearest you. Once you have finished, go and personally visit all ten operators you listed and tell them about how, by combining your purchasing power, you are going to save them a lot of money on their printing.

113. Get quotes for pre-printed forms

Printing your own invoices and statements with a laser or inkjet printer may be tempting, but is actually more expensive than purchasing pre-printed forms. After including the expense of your paper, toner or ink and labour—not to mention wear and tear on your printer or photocopier—see if your in-house production cost is more than what a printer would charge.

> *Sharon manages a very busy sales centre that raises funds for a number of charitable organisations. It was estimated that the sales office would use approximately 10 000 sales forms in a year. Initially, she believed it would be cheaper to photocopy the forms internally. However, having worked out the cost of doing this and then compared it to what a printer could provide, she was able to save her company $200 on the printing charges and close to $500 in staff time by having the sales forms printed externally.*

114. Annual report savings

Most company annual reports are an absolute work of art—a masterpiece in the making. To me, this is a real contradiction, as a key element of any annual report is to outline the financial performance of the organisation and yet most businesses go out of their way to spend a small fortune putting their annual report together. And who reads them? In my experience, hardly anyone! Most annual reports are either thrown in the rubbish soon after they are received, or condemned to a lonely, dusty existence sitting on a bookshelf or in some filing cabinet. In many cases, boxes of unused copies don't even get to see the light of day outside the storeroom.

> *Allan had just been appointed director of operations for a medium-sized building and construction firm, and one of his first duties was to oversee the production of the company annual report. After looking at samples of the previous years' reports and their hefty budgets,*

he concluded that the process was far too expensive and time-consuming. He cut down on the quality and amount of colour in the cover, used no colour within the report, dramatically reduced the number of photos and kept the content to a minimum of 500 words per section. Large savings were also made by not hiring an artist, existing photographs were recycled saving on photography expenses, and a member of the public relations staff undertook the copywriting functions. The combined effect of these strategies was significantly reduced printing costs from a more scaled-down but no less effective report. He then looked at past recipients of the report and determined that many of the organisations and individuals could be deleted from the list. These included competing businesses, organisations that had previously sought sponsorship or donations from his company, and students who had requested information for a university project. By almost halving the distribution list, Allan was also able to make further savings on printing costs, as well as on postage and handling charges by not having to send out so many copies.

CHAPTER 5

POSTAGE, COURIERS AND CONTACT DETAILS

Even though we live in an age of technological boom, the postal system still provides a vital and reliable service for many businesses. Whether you use it for daily communication, generating sales or collecting revenue, the strategies in this chapter will help your business save money in an area where it is normally difficult to reduce costs. Economical and practical tips for the use of couriers are also included, plus ideas for updating your all-important customer base.

courier

Chapter 5

Postage, couriers and contact details

This chapter covers:

Cut expenses on postage and couriers

Ever since the early days of the Pony Express, we have relied on postal service for our personal and professional needs. Even in this era of computers and the super highway we are still reliant on the mail, but are becoming increasingly aware that postal and courier charges can be a major expense. Your postage expenses are another area where the smallest of charges can soon add up. The following strategies will help your mail get through every single time, and for less.

115. Post office assistance

If in doubt—ask! The staff at your local post office can provide you with a wealth of information on how to save costs for your business. Specifically, they can give you information on mailing rates and charges, bulk mail, periodicals and overseas mail, as well as provide you with brochures, booklets and other printed material that you can take away and study. If you don't ask, then you don't get.

116. Australia Post services to save you money

The other day I received a brochure in the mail outlining some of the services that Australia Post can offer businesses to save both time and money. Here is just a selection.

Express Post

Save on expensive overnight courier costs by using Australia Post's excellent overnight service, Express Post. This is an efficient and relatively inexpensive express postal service that can be used for sending documents and other information. If posted before 6 pm, your package is guaranteed to reach most major cities the very next day. Conditions do apply for deliveries to certain regional areas, so check with the post office staff first. Bulk purchase discounts are also available, saving you even more money, and some of the packs have no weight restrictions. I use this service extensively, especially for important or urgent documents, as your parcel is tracked by the postal service every step of its journey, from the time it leaves your hands to the time the postman delivers it to your customer's letterbox.

Bulk savings

Australia Post offers discounts for bulk postage that is pre-sorted by postcode. It may only be a few cents per item but it all adds up over a year, especially if you do regular large mailings.

Register your publication

If your organisation produces a regular newsletter or magazine that you post to a large database, you may want to consider having the publication registered with Australia Post. This service will guarantee you substantial postal savings.

Direct discounts

Want to promote your newest activity, program or event? Look no further than your postal service. Australia Post has excellent direct mail discounts where, if you send 300 or more identical, personalised mail pieces, you can save up to 35 per cent of your direct mailing costs. Now that's worth considering.

All-in-one mailing

Sometimes it makes more sense to have someone give you a hand to send out your direct mail pieces. Australia Post provides a service that prepares and mails your invoices, letters and direct mail pieces, saving you time and money.

Unaddressed savings

This is a great way for you to target mail drops to homes, businesses or post boxes in specific locations, and it is particularly good for direct response marketing. Have you got a special offer that you want to promote? Then consider the Unaddressed Delivery Service (UDS).

117. When one gram saved me $1000

The size and weight of your postal item can have a dramatic effect on your mailing costs. In some cases, a matter of grams can make a huge difference to your bottom line.

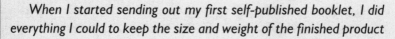

When I started sending out my first self-published booklet, I did everything I could to keep the size and weight of the finished product

down to a minimum. The publication was printed double-sided with a lightweight plastic spiral binding; thin card was used for the back cover and a clear plastic sheet for the front. I included just two sheets of paper—a cover letter and a tax invoice—along with a C4 envelope, and that was my mailing piece. All up this cost me $1.47 per unit to post anywhere in Australia. One day I accidentally printed the invoice on the back of the cover letter and realised that maybe I should continue to do this as it would save paper. Most people throw away the cover letter anyway, so all I would need to do was mention that the invoice was printed on the reverse side of the letter. When I went to the post office I got a big surprise—the postage for my new, lighter package was only 98c! I was told this was because the package was one gram lighter and thus in the lower postal rate. On the current level of sales of this publication, I plan to save over $1000 a year on the postage costs.

118. Design cost-effective mail pieces

Before designing your promotional and direct mail pieces, ensure that you or your designer is aware of the postal regulations that will impact on mailing costs. Your postal charges can be excessive for items that don't lie flat or qualify for postal automation. They will also be more expensive if items are larger than the accepted standard sizes set by the post office.

Stuart saved his business over $5000 in a year by changing the design of their mailing pieces. The original item put together by a graphic design firm was a professional production that was A5 size. Stuart took the sample down to the post office and discovered that it was going to cost over $1.50 per item to send—too expensive for the intended distribution of over 10 000. He asked the post office staff for a few suggestions and then went back to the design team to make some changes. They reduced the size of the finished item from A5 to cheque book size so it would fit into the standard envelopes that the company already had in stock, saving extra costs as new envelopes would not have to be printed.

As an alternative, you could use postcards rather than letters or other forms of direct mail pieces. You will save on printing costs, envelopes and the time to stuff each mail piece. Always check the potential costs first, because it is too late to make changes once everything is printed.

119. Take everything to the post office

There are only two ways to ensure that you are paying the correct postage for your mail. The first is to take everything to the post office, though this can be time consuming for the busy small business operator. The second method is to get a rate chart from the post office and weigh each item at your home or office. There is nothing more frustrating than seeing staff slap four 50c stamps on an envelope when the actual postage is only $1.67—that's an extra 33c you're paying. To eliminate over stamping, keep a variety of stamp denominations on hand. If you are regularly sending mail pieces that are the same size and weight, know what the charges are and have the appropriate combination of stamps. I use a food scale to measure the weight of my packages. I then cross-reference the weight against the rate chart and apply the appropriate stamps. Quick, simple and it takes all the guesswork out of sending your mail. And it's a strategy that's saved me a lot of money. However, keep stamps in a secure place, as leaving them lying around the office is an open invitation to pilferage from staff: I once had an employee who used twenty stamps from the office supply to send personal Christmas cards.

120. Bundle it together and send once

If your business sends many pieces of mail to the same destination on a regular basis, accumulate a day's mailing and send it in one large envelope. This will eliminate having to pay separate postage for each individual item. Clearly indicate the name of the recipient on each item inside the envelope to facilitate distribution at the other end.

When I was based in Brisbane we regularly sent mail such as employment and taxation forms, invoices and reports to our head office in Sydney. Unless the item was urgent, we would save everything until Friday then stick it all in one envelope. We chose Friday because it would always be guaranteed to get there on Monday. By sending everything together we saved around $2 a time and, given that we did this every week, around $100 a year on this one postage item alone.

121. Post-office boxes

Many small business operators find value in renting a PO box for $50 to $150 a year. However, don't rush out and get yourself a PO box simply because you think it will add a professional touch to your business. On the contrary, a PO box doesn't necessarily present a positive image of your business, as it can be perceived as impersonal in the eyes of customers and also lacks the identity of a street address. PO box addresses are also widely used by many shonky business operators, especially in the direct marketing industry, and may therefore suggest that your business is unstable. In addition, you also have to spend time and money going to the post office every day to check your mail.

If you do decide to go for a PO box, be sure to choose one that suits your needs. The post office has a number of different sizes priced accordingly. Work out how much mail you will be receiving and opt for the best size box. In my experience, most small business operators can get by with the smallest size PO box—though don't forget to clear it daily.

122. Email, fax or phone

Not that I want to do all those nice people at the post office out of a job, but you should try to make postage your last resort. The best way to save on postage is to avoid it altogether. If possible, send documents by email or fax as they are much cheaper. Or better still, if you can resolve an issue with a quick phone call or in person then do it. Not only are email, fax and phone a lot quicker and more efficient, they will also save you time and money.

123. On time, overnight—we deliver

Sometimes even your best-laid plans can go awry and you suddenly need to have something delivered across town or interstate, and it should have been there yesterday. This is when the courier company comes to your rescue. Couriers are a necessary evil that have risen to popularity due to our lack of organisational skills, our need for instantaneous gratification and our reliance on the word 'urgent'. Nonetheless, couriers do have a role to play and they have saved my hide on many occasions. Consider the following ideas before you next book a courier, as they will save your bank account as well as your hide.

Shop around

If you use couriers regularly, spend some time getting quotes from a wide range of different companies. The difference in price can be considerable—through shopping around, I was able to save my business up to $40 a job (see Chapter 1).

What service do you require?

Many couriers offer different levels of service—standard or express. Express is much more expensive. Know the difference and educate staff, as there is no point being overserviced. When making a booking with the courier company, ensure you state what service you require. If the level of service required is not mentioned by the customer, then many couriers will charge you for the faster service at a higher rate.

Get coordinated

Coordinate with other businesses in your area to use the same courier service and negotiate a cheaper corporate rate.

Get it right

Ensure that your employees are getting the correct delivery details of the customer. This not only includes specific address details, but also specific delivery instructions. Confirm the time and day of collection with the customer, as couriers will often charge you for a call-out when there are 'no goods to go'.

DIY courier

Perhaps you or your staff can deliver some items instead of using a courier. Will you be passing a customer's premises on your way home or to a meeting? If so, it doesn't take long to drop something off yourself. Not only will you save a lot of money but you can be guaranteed that the packages have been delivered. Your customers will also appreciate the personal service.

Get organised

Avoid having to send documents by overnight courier by getting organised. If you know you have a deadline to meet, complete the task early so as to leave plenty of time to send the information by normal post. And as with regular mail, if you have a number of items to go to the same destination bundle them together, or delay them by a day or two (if it suits the customer) so that you can coordinate deliveries.

124. Go international

If you have to send items internationally, consult the post office first. A few months ago I had to send a package to Malaysia. I consulted the three main international courier companies and was quoted between $140 and $160 for delivery. At the post office I discovered that the same package could be sent for only $40 and it would take three to five days to be delivered. This was fine with me as time was not that important. The irony of this situation is that the post office uses the same courier company that was going to charge me $160.

125. Sending stuff overseas

Ask yourself whether it is worth keeping the international addresses on your mailing list. Of course, if they are regular customers and are purchasing your products then they should remain. However, if you are just sending them information because they found their way onto your database by filling out a registration form at a trade show, I suggest scrapping them immediately. Alternatively, look for cheaper ways such as email to send them information, as international postage costs are at least double local rates. You would be better off spending this money marketing to potential local prospects than sending it to someone who will probably never buy your products.

Keep contact details up-to-date

Having worked in direct marketing for many years, I truly know the importance of keeping the contact details of your customers updated. Many businesses employ database management firms to update their customer listings once a year. Here are some ideas that will mean you will never have to hire one of these firms again— and you'll save on wasted mail costs.

126. Return to sender, address unknown!

Hardly music to the ears of any small business owner, these words mean more money flushed down the drain. Every time I receive one of our mailings with 'Return to sender' or 'Not at this address' emblazoned across the envelope, I cringe. But keeping your database updated is not such a daunting task as long as you make it a regular part of your working day. The easiest place to start to update your customer list is by calling the customer every time you receive a return mail piece. Track them down and get their updated contact information, including at least three contact phone numbers: home, business and mobile. Be sure to inform colleagues who have the same person's details of any changes.

127. Tell us when you move

Moving house or office is a pain, not least due to having to notify everyone about the change of address. When I moved from Brisbane to Sydney I set about contacting everyone I could think of with my new address details—family, friends, colleagues, customers, my bank, my accountant and the tax department. I thought I had basically covered everyone until I started receiving forwarded mail from a wide range of organisations that I had totally forgotten about. Make it easy for your customers to remember to notify you of any address change. Choose one or more of the following to place a change of address form.

- on the back of your envelopes
- in your customer newsletter
- on your website
- on your invoices
- inside all correspondence
- as a postscript to all your emails and letters.

In this way it will be virtually impossible for your customers not to remember you when they move.

128. Make updating part of your customer service

The easiest, most up-to-date and cost-effective method of keeping your database accurate is by making updating a normal part of every contact you have with your customers. Whenever a member calls our customer service line we use this as an opportunity to update their contact details—it only takes a minute and the majority of customers don't mind. Deal with the customer inquiry first and once this has been resolved, confirm the contact details.

129. When your customers send you information

When you receive correspondence from a customer, cross-reference the contact information with that on your database. I have found many customers do not give out alternative contact details, but these are quickly entered into the database when a customer sends us a note written on their business letterhead.

130. Merge and purge your database frequently

At least once a year print out your customer listing by surname and then check it for duplicate entries. Scan down the list and look for irregularities such as entries with the same first and last name or the same initial for their first name. Then go into your database and cross-reference these by address and phone numbers to see if they are the same person. If they are, contact the customer and ask them which entry they would like to keep and then delete the others. This is particularly important if you have set up a mailing list of potential customers. I have been on the receiving end of four identical pieces of mail from one organisation. They all had different variations of my name and company details and that company had wasted $1.50 on postage, printing and handling to send those duplicate copies to me—and doubtless to numerous others too.

6

TELEPHONE AND FAX

Every small business owes a large debt to Alexander Graham Bell. His invention of the telephone created an efficient avenue of communication that, if used properly, can be your biggest ally in business. If abused, it can also become your biggest expense. The following tips will enable you to maximise the use of the telephone within your business while minimising its cost.

Chapter 6

Telephone and fax

This chapter covers:

131. Compare prices

There is no better time than now to shop around for your telecommunications provider. There are so many companies in the marketplace that you have plenty of options when considering telephone, mobile phone and Internet requirements. The downside is that trying to choose what is best for you can get confusing. You need to ensure you are getting the most cost-effective provider that can best meet your specific needs. To do this, first write down your specific telephone requirements—these would include the number of phone lines you require, how many local, STD and international calls you make per month, approximately how long the average call goes for and at what time of day most calls occur. As for your mobile phone, will you mainly receive calls or also make a lot of calls from it? Will you need to make international calls or local and interstate only? Once you have listed all your requirements, write down how each telecommunications provider rates in accordance with price and service. This will give you an overview of what everyone is offering and enable you to make a more informed decision based on your needs, not theirs. Try to review your telecommunication rates at least once a year to ensure you are still getting the best deal possible.

132. Long-distance savings

Sometimes it is far more effective to speak with someone about a particular matter than communicate by fax, email or post. So if you need to make international or STD calls or send faxes, try to call during off-peak times (usually between 7 pm and 7 am) as the rates are much cheaper. Some phone companies have fantastic deals whereby you can chat to someone interstate for half an hour or more after 7 pm and pay less than a couple of dollars. In some cases, the time difference will mean that you can take advantage of these after-hours savings and still be able to reach the other person during their working hours.

Keep an eye out for promotions being run by phone companies. One phone company recently ran a promotion for STD calls at only 1c a minute to anywhere in Australia on a Saturday. What a fantastic deal! Judy, who operates her own successful network marketing business, decided not to let such a great opportunity slip by. She arranged times via email with her top ten distributors and called them individually on Saturday to conduct a one-hour training and *business development session. Judy was able to inspire and motivate ten of her colleagues who were located all over the country for a measly $6.*

What could you do to add value to your business and take advantage of future telephone savings? The next time you see a great offer like Judy did, consider implementing any of the following strategies.

■ Run a fax promotion.

■ Make a courtesy call to some customers you know work on Saturdays.

■ Make calls to prospective customers.

■ Chase up overdue accounts from regional areas or interstate.

■ Hold a personal one-to-one training session with staff.

■ Call those old customers who haven't bought anything from you for some time.

133. Bar STD calls

Unless it is absolutely necessary for your business, ensure STD and IDD calls cannot be made from your phones. If you occasionally require these services, assign your own office phone as the dedicated long-distance line. Or make the fax machine the only phone in the office that has international call access, so if you see anyone on the fax/phone you can be fairly sure they are making an IDD call.

An alternative way of preventing abuse of STD lines is to subscribe to have an 'STD bar' set up on all your phones. This system allows you to lock each phone, preventing any long-distance calls being made. By simply entering a personal ID code into the phone, you can lock all your phones during lunch breaks and at the end of each day. The cost of doing this is minimal compared to the potential losses that could be incurred from unauthorised use.

Wayne operates a medium-sized equipment hire business that leases out construction and maintenance machinery to businesses and individuals within regional New South Wales and Northern Victoria. His business makes and receives many STD calls to and from these areas. Wayne has a cleaner that comes in to tidy the office and workshop area three times a week. While going through his telephone bill one month, Wayne noticed that a call was being placed to the same number after office hours. He discovered that the cleaner had been calling his girlfriend who was living in a town some four hundred kilometres away. Wayne went back through all the phone bills for the period the cleaner had been employed and realised that over $220 worth of calls had been made. The cost of subscribing to a service that would allow him to lock his phones from making long-distance calls would have been less than $20 over the same period.

134. Personal savings

It's a given that employees will have a need to make phone calls from work to deal with personal issues from time to time. Obviously, employees should not be making unlimited personal calls, but the occasional call kept short shouldn't be considered a problem. Try not to get too absorbed in trying to catch out employees making personal calls. There's a fine line between the cost of the telephone charges incurred and the cost of the time you have wasted in trying to police the situation vigilantly. Therefore, a certain degree of trust must exist. Here are some ideas you can implement to prevent abuse by employees.

- Develop a telephone policy for your business and include it as part of your employees' handbook.

- Check phone bills to spot any abuse.

- Bar international calls from all phones.

- If you do catch someone abusing the system, take appropriate action and ensure the call charges are reimbursed immediately. Ensure other employees are aware of what has happened.

- Employees should be asked to identify long-distance calls on an honour system.

- If your employees are making a large number of personal calls at work, it may not be the cost of the local call that could be hurting your business. It's more likely the fact that the staff member is neglecting their work; for instance, your customers are probably not receiving the level of service they should, so they don't come back. How many times have you walked into a store only to find a shop assistant chatting on the phone to a friend and totally oblivious to your presence?

A bigger threat to your phone bill is when employees make lengthy long-distance or international calls. An employee should be expected to pay for any charges incurred by making these calls. This is not an unreasonable expectation and most employees shouldn't have a problem paying for their personal long-distance calls.

Problems arise when employees overstep the boundaries of trust that have been established and flagrantly abuse the use of company telephones to make their personal international calls. Edgar was a sales manager for a medium-sized promotions company and had visions of moving up within the business. He also had a girlfriend who was living in South America. In this particular instance, absence certainly made the heart grow fonder for Edgar because he couldn't resist the temptation to call his loved one using the company phone. The financial controller carried out a spot check of the phone bills and noticed in excess of $600 worth of calls placed to the same number in South America. When approached about the matter Edgar said he was going to speak to someone in the company about it but had forgotten!

Don't leave anything to chance in your business. It could cost you dearly.

135. Directory savings

I once received a telephone bill for my company only to find that we had been charged for 245 phone calls made to directory assistance. Upon further investigation I found out the calls had been made by employees who were too lazy to look up the number in the telephone book. Staff commented that there were not enough phone books, so I went straight to the post office and got one copy of the white and yellow pages phone books for each employee. If you have ever tried to get through to directory assistance, you will agree that in many cases it is quicker to use the phone book than wait in a queue because 'all the lines are currently busy'. That's hardly saving you time or money! Did you know it could cost you upwards of 40c per call to directory assistance? And if you use the Call Connect service that puts you straight through without actually telling you the telephone number for future reference, it's around 90c a call.

A cheaper alternative is to use the white and yellow pages on the Internet. The website addresses for these two services are kept in my Favourites folder for easy reference and are www.whitepages.com.au and www.yellowpages.com.au. Citysearch is also a handy reference tool: www.citysearch.com.au. Also, avoid pricey telephone services such as the National Operator and Missed Call Retrieval.

136. Call toll free

In an effort to provide greater customer service and increase sales, many businesses now have a toll-free number. Save on your phone charges by calling these free numbers whenever possible. Make sure you have the toll-free 1-800 or 1-300 numbers for all the suppliers, vendors, contractors and other people you regularly do business with. If a customer has a toll-free number, record it as their main contact number; if you don't have their number, then check their product catalogue, latest invoice, the phone book or their website. Even greater savings can be made if your suppliers or customers are regional or interstate, as you will avoid having to pay long-distance charges.

If your company has its own toll-free number, ensure you manage it well to cut costs. Call charges to these lines are considerably higher for the receiver of the call than those to normal phone lines.

137. Extra phone lines

Do you know exactly how many phone lines your business has or needs? If you are not using some phone lines, have them disconnected straight away as they are costing you money. Even though no calls are being charged, you are still being slugged for the line rental that can be in excess of $30 per month per line. Just one dormant line will cost your business over $350 per year. Alternatively, look at ways of using one line for a number of different functions in order to cut the number of telephone lines you have.

Nigel operates his own successful financial planning business and his small team consists of an office manager and two financial planners, who are normally out on the road for most of the day attending appointments. By his own admission, Nigel's office was overserviced *with telephone lines. In addition to the main line for the office manager, there were four other telephone lines, two fax lines and four separate lines for Internet access. He had a total of eleven lines for his small operation. As very few faxes were sent or received, Nigel immediately deleted one fax line altogether, as well as two of the other telephone lines. It was extremely rare that Nigel and his two planners were in the office at the same time doing administration work, so they could easily manage to share the remaining two phones. Two separate Internet connections were kept as separate lines while the other two lines were disconnected completely. If the staff or Nigel required Internet access, they piggybacked on the telephone or fax line. Customers were still able to call in as the main line was kept free. By making these few changes Nigel was able to save himself over $1700 a year in telephone line rental alone.*

By combining multiple services such as Internet, telephone and fax on the same line, you can save yourself a considerable amount of money. Of course, if you are using a dial-up service you cannot use multiple services at the same time, but broadband services enable you to use one phone line simultaneously for multiple purposes. In one sales office I managed we combined the fax, Internet and credit card terminal all on the one line, saving over $700 a year on line rental.

138. Check your phone bills religiously

Always get a complete itemised copy of your telephone bill then check the following items.

■ Ensure you are only being charged for the phone lines you are using. I know of a number of businesses that were charged for phone lines that were not even theirs.

■ Compare the number and types of calls being made to ensure that your employees are not making excessive calls to directory assistance, Call Connect and other network features.

■ Look at the time and day that calls are being made—if there are calls made during lunch hour and after normal operating hours, there is a good chance that your staff or someone else may be making personal calls during these times.

■ Check the number of STD and mobile phone calls being made and the phones from which the largest number of these calls are made. This will assist you in spotting any possible abuses by specific employees.

■ Look for a larger than normal amount of calls being made to the same phone number from the same line. In many cases this is an indication of personal calls being made.

If something appears on your phone bill that you are not sure about, query it with the phone company. I found an item on my phone bill that said 'Other calls', charging $5.50 for five calls. I contacted the phone company and they informed me that it was for a new form of directory assistance service they provided. I immediately advised all employees not to use this service and we have not received a similar charge since.

139. Mobile savings

We now live in an 'instantaneous' society where the advent of modern technology such as the mobile phone has meant we expect everything to happen immediately. Don't fall victim to false pressures and marketing hype, and you will save yourself a ton of money. I know many business people, myself included, who operate successfully without the use of a mobile phone.

Iain is one such small business operator. As director of his own successful training company, Iain spends three-quarters of his time conducting powerful training programs for all types of small businesses. A large proportion of his remaining working week is spent making sales presentations to potential clients. In both instances, if Iain did have a mobile phone then no one could contact him anyway because he would have it switched off out of professional courtesy—something that seems to deteriorate as soon as someone acquires a mobile phone. You can call Iain's office at any time of the day and if he is not there, Jean, his highly competent office manager, is able to take a message and Iain ensures he returns the call at the earliest possible time.

I will only ever call someone on their mobile if it is an absolute emergency—in other words, if I am about to lose a major client or my business or I could end up in prison. In my experience, one of the following three things tends to happen when you call someone on their mobile.

■ You can't get through to them anyway.

■ They can't talk because they are in a meeting, doing something important, driving or surrounded by background noise.

■ They will probably ask if they can call you when they get back to the office because the information you require is sitting on their desk.

If the mobile phone number is the only contact you have for a client, supplier or potential customer, call them and ask if there is a landline such as an office number that you could call them right back on. This will save you money on phone charges and there is also less chance that your call will be disconnected due to a flat mobile phone battery or bad reception.

Does every one of your employees who has a mobile phone provided by your business really need one? If your staff rarely leave the office, don't travel very much or are not on call after hours, they should not need a mobile phone—and it is likely the phone's main use is for calling or texting their friends.

140. Use SMS instead

Another thing about mobile phones that irks me is the advent of the text messaging service (SMS) or texting. Unfortunately, what is potentially a brilliant piece of communication technology has turned many people into brainless, self-absorbed textaholics. However, I admit that, if used properly, the SMS service can afford considerable savings for your business. As it is much cheaper than a mobile phone call, you will save on phone bill charges. Here are a few ways you can effectively use your SMS service to save time and money:

■ to confirm a meeting with a client or potential customer

■ to wish a customer a happy birthday

■ to thank a customer or supplier

■ to send a message to existing customers about a new product or promotion you are running.

141. Pre-paid calling cards

Whether you are travelling locally or overseas, it is always cheaper to use a pre-paid calling card. When living in the Philippines, my wife and I would call home on a regular basis. We were paying an absolute fortune for these calls until we discovered the pre-paid calling card. It literally saved us thousands of dollars over a year.

142. Make your fax go faster

Simplicity is the answer when sending faxes. People willingly accept a lesser quality production by fax, enabling your business to maximise its use as an effective communication and marketing tool. The cost of sending faxes can be heavily reduced by adopting the following strategies.

Minimise design elements

Reduce the time it takes for your fax page to be sent by reducing the amount of graphics, bold print, large headings and shaded areas used. This is particularly relevant if you are sending faxes on a long-distance call. While these features may look great, they can add minutes to the time it takes for your fax to go through and also require more toner to be used by the receiving fax. I have often requested companies to fax me information about their business and products, only to have an almost illegible document come through because they had faxed their full-colour glossy brochure complete with photos and fancy graphics. If you are in this situation, spend half an hour transferring the important information onto a one-page fax using your computer, and when a customer requests a fax, simply print one off and away you go.

Never use colour

As obvious as this may sound I know of a number of businesses that produce information on a colour printer for the specific purpose of sending it by fax. It still comes out the other end in black and white, so save your printer toner and reduce your fax time by printing in black.

Use white paper only

Keep order forms on white paper to make it easier to send, receive and read.

I recently received a direct mail item for business-related training programs. To make the order form stand out from the rest of the package, the company had printed it on blue paper. The order encouraged respondents to send it back via fax by highlighting the return fax number in large bold type. The problem was, when you filled out the form and faxed it back it was very difficult to read. As a result the training company spent a number of hours chasing up potential customers and asking them to resend their order on a white order form.

143. Do away with fax cover sheets and reports

You can save on both fax charges and paper costs by doing away completely with your fax cover sheet and combining the contact information and message all on one page. Keep the header and contact details to a minimum in terms of the information provided, the size of the print and the spacing. This should not take up more than one fifth of the page, thereby maximising the space available for your message. You can also experiment with using smaller font size and margins to fit everything on the one page. And if you have only a short message to send, cut off any blank paper and just send the part with the written text.

One of the other major areas of waste when faxing are the transmission reports that provide you with a print-out of all faxes sent and received and their status. Unless it is crucial to your business to have proof that every single fax went through, then do away with these reports altogether. All fax machines have a digital display panel and a signal tone at the end of transmission to indicate if the transmission was a success—these should be sufficient. Some businesses have the transmission report print out after every fax, only to throw it in the bin once they have checked it—what a waste of paper. If you do need a copy, set the report to print out at the end of each week or after twenty faxes have been sent or received.

144. Purchase new models that do more

Make technology work for you. Newer model faxes have features such as quick scanning for delayed transmission, dual access that allows for sending and receiving simultaneously and automatic redialling and resending capabilities. You just have to put in the fax, punch in the number, press send and walk away. If you are currently using one of those old dinosaur faxes that use thermal paper and you have to photocopy the faxes received to make a more permanent copy, get rid of it and upgrade to a newer model. You'll save costs through not having to purchase thermal paper, no more photocopying expenses plus the time spent having to do this. While email has become the prime technology of choice for long-distance communication, many businesses are still sending documents by fax. If you have several faxes to send to the same number then save them and fax everything at the same time rather than individually. The reason behind this is that many international calls incur a connection fee, or flag fall, and then charge for every minute onwards. By sending faxes together you will pay only one connection fee.

7

COMPUTERS, TECHNOLOGY AND OFFICE EQUIPMENT

The correct use of technology in your business will make your life simpler and more productive. It should only be used if it is going to save you time and money. And you don't have to be a computer nerd to make technology work for you. Here are some simple ways in which technology can save your business a great deal of time and money.

Chapter 7

Computers, technology and office equipment

This chapter covers:

145. Get connected

Send as much correspondence and conduct as much business over the Internet as possible. There has never been a cheaper, more efficient and more flexible method of communicating than by email. I cannot remember the last time I sent a letter or memo 'the good old-fashioned way' since I became Internet and email literate. Here are some useful tips for effective use of email.

■ Keep emails short and simple—the conventions of letter writing do not apply.

■ Proofread everything before sending.

■ Spelling and grammar are still important—email is not an excuse for sloppy communication, especially in business.

■ An email is not always the best option—a phone call can sometimes be more efficient.

■ Know when and how often the recipient checks their email, and send your message accordingly.

The efficiency of email makes it a popular and ideal business tool. However, it is this very characteristic that can also cause it to be a burden on your time. Because email is so easy to use, your inbox can end up with hundreds of messages, many unnecessary, and you waste a great deal of time sorting through them. Here are a few more handy hints to keep your email working for you.

■ Only send a message if you really need to.

■ Be selective who you send your message to—don't just copy it to everyone.

■ Don't send large attachments to groups of people, as it will take forever to send and waste your time.

■ Keep your business and personal email addresses separate—there is a time and place for everything.

■ Install a quarantine system that prevents your email from receiving certain types of messages. My office computer blocks any message attachments with the extension 'EXE' or 'VBS'. This saves me time and frustration, as I don't have to read through a whole pile of unwanted junk email. As soon as I see the subject heading High Risk Attachment Blocked, I delete the message immediately.

146. Save off-line and on-line

Internet rental charges come in many shapes and sizes but they basically fall into two types. The first is where you pay a minimum monthly rental that allows you a set amount of time on-line each month. You are charged if you use more than the allocated time. The second option is where you pay a flat monthly rate that gives you unlimited time on-line.

If your Internet account falls into the first category, then you can save on your Internet charges by doing all your work off-line. Once all the documents have been completed to your satisfaction then log on and send them. I am amazed when I see people composing messages on-line and invariably they have to answer the phone or attend to a customer, an employee or a host of other distractions, and a two-minute email turns into a one-hour Internet bill. Many Internet services now have a function that automatically disconnects after a set time period if it has not been used. If you find that you are very close to exceeding your monthly allocation of Internet time, see what projects requiring the Internet you can leave until next month.

Alternatively, unlimited monthly Internet usage for a set fee is a very attractive option but beware of the hidden costs. Every time you connect to the Internet you are charged the cost of a local call. Now I didn't consider this to be much of an expense until I reviewed my phone bills over a six-month period. I discovered that on average I logged on fifteen times in the course of a day. In many cases, this was just a few minutes to check or send an email. If I reduced this to only five times a day, I would effectively reduce my phone bill by approximately $780 a year (10 less calls per day x 30 cents per call x 5 days per week x 52 weeks in a year). Remember, profit is in the detail.

Another alternative is to subscribe to a broadband Internet connection. This high-speed connection to your Internet service provider enables your email to register in your Inbox the moment it arrives, without the cost and time required to dial up a connection. While more expensive than the normal service, it can save you time and money in the long run.

147. Pay your bills on-line

Have a look at all your expenses and determine whether you can pay any of these via the Internet. All banks now provide the facilities for you to transfer money from your account to someone else's, even if it is with a different bank. If you don't have this facility set up for your accounts already, give your bank a call today or go and see them in person. Utility companies such as telephone and power services also enable you to pay your bills direct on-line. Making payments over the Internet is a convenient way to save you time and postage.

Many customers of my direct mail business prefer to deposit payment into my bank account via the Internet because it is quick, easy and far more cost-effective. A number of my publications cost under $20, so many customers consider it wasteful to use a credit card or write a cheque/money order for such a small amount. They simply log on to the Internet, transfer the funds on-line and then email or fax me the confirmation report. I then go on-line and check my account to verify the deposit has been made.

148. Save against technology losses

Regardless of whether you are a small business or a multimillion-dollar international corporation, you must protect yourself against loss of productivity from computer downtime. Many businesses have become so reliant on computers and other technology that a technological problem can be devastating.

When I first began my direct mail publishing business, I leased a brand new computer as I couldn't afford to buy one outright. The sales person also offered me some very affordable antivirus software that would have set me back just over $100, but I decided against it, believing (or hoping!) that I wouldn't need it and could save a few bucks without it. Well, six months into the business my computer crashed after catching a virus of bubonic proportions. It took three weeks and a considerable amount of money to get everything up and running again, and restore all the vital information that had been lost. As a result, I lost nearly 10 per cent of my business's gross annual revenue.

I learnt the hard way but this experience taught me there are some very simple steps all business owners can take to protect themselves against such potentially damaging loss.

Install antivirus software

Install antivirus software on all your computers and make sure you keep it updated. Don't suffer the same fate that I did for the sake of trying to save a few bucks. Antivirus software is the most effective prevention against email virus infection. Two of the most popular antivirus systems are by McAfee and Symantec.

Keep saving documents

Set your computer to save the document you are working on every few minutes (Tools > Options > Save, then tick the box 'Save AutoRecover info every [5] minutes'). This will ensure any changes to your documents will be saved as you work. You never know when you are going to get distracted and have to leave your computer to do something else. If an employee needs to use the computer, they may exit your document without saving your work and all the changes will be lost.

Back up your work

Do this every single day. It should be standard operating procedure for your business to back up information at least once a day. If the work is of significant importance, more regular backups should occur. It is wise to keep a backup on the hard drive plus one on floppy disk; when I was working on this book I kept a backup of each chapter on a separate floppy disk and on my computer hard drive. If any of the disks became corrupted, I would only lose one chapter and not the whole book, and I would have a spare I could revert to on the computer.

Use a surge protector

Save against surges and sags in power by using a surge protector connected to all your electronic equipment. These relatively inexpensive devices will absorb any major variances in power and prevent your computer from 'blowing up'. I remember in my final year at uni busily typing out my thesis report in the computer lab, when all of a sudden the room lights flickered and the computer screen went blank. There had been a massive power surge to the building and all the computers had been fried, along with 9322 words of my required 10 000-word thesis! And I had not backed up to a floppy disk.

Use passwords

Use passwords to limit access to your computer. In many cases, employees infect computers with viruses through indiscriminate personal use. Set up security measures so that the user must enter a password to gain access to any of the programs; without this password the computer cannot be used.

149. When buying a computer, look for only the features you need

When purchasing a computer for your organisation, don't get sucked into buying a super high-tech machine that has all sorts of great functions—functions you will never ever use! Not only are you spending more money than you need to, this new technology takes a significant amount of time to learn and at the end of the day, it may not add any further value to your business over what you are already using.

It's difficult not to get sucked in by those fancy space-age designs that have become synonymous with the latest model of computers. While they look great, this cosmetic marketing will invariably cost you extra dollars for little or no extra benefits. This is what Felicia had to contend with in her small corporate firm. The girls working in administration wanted to purchase four new flat screen computers valued at around $3000 each. In justifying their request, no mention was made as to how these new computers would increase productivity, save time or enable them to provide a better service to their clients. Instead, they said the new computers looked more 'corporate' and would blend in better with the existing office decor. The computers would have set Felicia back $12 000 just to make four desks look good.

Compare also the estimated productivity savings of any software upgrades with the total cost of installation, training and relearning the latest version. Waste abounds when your employees are continually learning new features and interfaces that look cool but have low incremental productivity value. A good example is the release of Microsoft Office 2000. Many of my computer-savvy friends, including one who conducts computer training courses, believe the practical advantages of the new version are inconsequential for most ordinary users. Many businesses spent hundreds or even thousands of dollars upgrading from Version 98 with very little benefit. When it comes to computers, trying to keep up with the Joneses will cost you a fortune on features you will hardly ever use. Yet some upgrades can save you money. For instance, your PC's performance can be increased with an inexpensive RAM upgrade. By increasing your RAM capacity, you can get a longer life out of your existing PC rather than having to replace the whole machine for a newer model.

150. Don't buy more technology than you need

In today's technology-driven world it's easy to get caught up in all the hype. Be careful not to go overboard when buying technology solutions that do not fit your business needs. Don't allow vendors to rush you into making a decision that might not be the right one for your business.

A friend of mine who I will call Fred (his name is an alias to protect him from further ridicule) started up a small accounting business. The first thing he needed to buy was office equipment, so he went to a major office technology supplier and within a few short hours the very slick salesperson had talked him into buying the latest model computer with more bells and whistles than he would ever use, a colour printer that any graphic designer would be proud to own, a scanner and a small office photocopier. He ended up paying about $5000 more than he really needed to, as the equipment he bought far exceeded his requirements. The moral of this story is pretty clear. Fred learned his lesson the hard way and I offered the salesman a job.

151. Create an on-line library resource

Avoid the heavy costs of printing manuals and the associated postage with this bright idea from the Hotel Dynamics Group.

HDG is the largest hotel loyalty marketing company in the world, and the market leader with over 100 sales offices in 35 countries. To ensure managers have immediate access to all the resources they need, the company has created an on-line library of relevant policies, procedures, manuals, publications, training ideas and management information that can be viewed at any time and from anywhere in the world. This facility also enables employees to stay in regular contact with each other via a discussion forum and the listing of weekly regional updates. As a result the company has realised considerable savings in printing and postage expenses, and in the reduction in long-distance telephone calls to access information that is now available on the website.

152. Realise huge savings with the Internet

With the advent of email and the Internet, opportunities abound for your business to provide information via these sources rather than in traditional paper format.

I recently received a copy of Association Times Online, *a publication targeting senior decision makers in the not-for-profit industry. It contained an article explaining how the Australian Spinal Research Foundation has saved almost $20 000 annually by using the Internet as a communication tool. The Foundation previously mailed a newsletter to 3000 chiropractors three times a year, at a cost of $2 each. The newsletter is now prepared as a pdf file which is attached to an email message. The article also described how Women's Golf Victoria previously printed and mailed updates of 20–30 pages to its 8000 club captains each month. The updates are now posted on its web page and club captains download from there. The savings are estimated to be $50 000 a year.*

If these two non-profit organisations can use the Internet to save themselves thousands of dollars and serve their customers better, what can you do in your business to achieve the same outcome? Here are just a few examples of items that your company can send by email, or post on the web or shared hard drive as appropriate:

- employees' payslips
- weekly reports
- contracts
- product information, price lists and quotes
- job proposals
- staff newsletters, bulletins and notices.

You can also request all job applications be received via email.

153. Reduce customer service expenses with the Internet

Do you have a web presence? More and more businesses are finding that the Internet can be used to reduce costs and free up employees' time to work on other revenue-generating activities. Websites can dramatically reduce your customer service costs by being a focal point for customer inquiries. I logged on to 100 small business websites and have put together the following list of 'must haves' for your own website.

- Include a feedback, question and answer or inquiries form that prospects or customers can complete on-line to receive a reply within 24 hours.

- Provide all the necessary information about your company background, products, key personnel and contact details, the latter on every page for convenience.

- Display products, pricing and availability information.

- If required, put a secured credit application on the site for customers to order via the Internet.

With regard to on-line sales, there is an initial cost in setting up your website and providing secure ordering and payment systems. However, the reduction in staffing, phone calls, mailing and printing costs might well be worth the initial expenditure. A web presence also enables you to open up new markets, especially regional and international ones, that you never thought possible. Just look at the success of on-line shopping sites such as eBay. My wife orders some facial products via the website of a well-known pharmaceutical company. It's ideal because it doesn't matter what part of the country or the world we are living in, she's able to get the products she needs quickly, safely and without hassle.

> *Frances is a successful executive coach who has realised just how beneficial a website can be for her consulting business. A new client based in France was recently surfing the Internet and came across Frances's website. She was so impressed by what she read that she signed up for a twelve-week program straight away. Frances now has an international business thanks to her presence on the Internet. No wonder they call it the World Wide Web.*

154. Technology can save you

The advancement of computer technology has extended well beyond that of the humble PC. Here are a few examples of how technology has benefited a number of small businesses.

Palm pilots and delivery businesses

Gone are the days when couriers or the deliverers of the office spring water gave you a paper invoice and asked you to sign a form as proof that you have received the goods. Electronic palm pilots are now all the rage and are providing considerable savings for businesses that have embraced this technology. The courier now records all transactions by scanning the collection receipt and capturing an electronic signature from the customer. With the press of a button the information is sent back to head office and stored into the customer's account file even before the courier gets out of your door. Orders are processed more quickly and staffing levels can be reduced as much of the work is done electronically.

Telephone advances and call centres

Technology is changing the face of many call centres and the way in which customers interact with them. Many are moving away from assisted service, where you talk to a consultant, to the convenience of self-help systems such as touch-phone and speech recognition. Automatic diallers have revolutionised outbound call centres by increasing the number of calls made, reducing down time between calls and leapfrogging engaged or disconnected numbers. Considerable savings in time and payroll have been realised along with a significant increase in productivity. However, while there are obvious savings to be gained from this system, businesses should also take into account its impersonal nature. In recent years there has been much consumer and media backlash against businesses which have implemented impersonal technological changes at the expense of providing personalised service to their customers.

Automatic receipts

When was the last time a taxi driver wrote you a manual receipt? Even the humble taxi driver has gone high-tech with the introduction of onboard electronic receipt machines. With the press of a few buttons a printed receipt is immediately produced, saving time for the driver and money on printing and distributing manual receipts for the taxi companies. Thanks to technology you can also get invoices and delivery notices printed out on the spot from couriers and delivery people. And gone are the days when you pay a bus fare directly to the driver. Now you walk up to a machine, insert a few coins and out pops your pre-paid ticket. The concept has also extended to auto-pay machines in car parks and other public places. The other day I wanted to make some photocopies at the public library so I purchased an electronic debit card by placing five dollars into a machine. Out popped my card and a GST invoice, and not a library employee in sight.

CD-ROMs for marketing purposes

I recently received a package in the mail from a property developer containing a CD-ROM and a brief cover note. I powered it up on my PC and was enthralled for the next three minutes as the images, background music and commentary got me very excited about retiring to a large villa complete with private jetty and swimming pool. I immediately contacted the realtor and inquired about the production of the CD-ROM (I'm not ready to retire just yet). He explained that such information was originally sent out in a paper prospectus that took considerable money, time and effort to print, bind and post. The CD-ROM is now the perfect alternative in a far more sophisticated and computer-savvy market. There is also much less cost and effort involved in creating the finished product.

155. Multifunction devices

Technology is such that you are now able to buy one machine that does an array of tasks. For instance, you can purchase a combined printer, copier, scanner, fax machine and telephone all in one space-saving unit. Better known as multifunction devices or MFDs, these modern technological wonders can enhance your business operations for as little as a few hundred dollars or as much as $20 000. And depending on your requirements, they significantly reduce the cost of setting up your office, save on space and limit the type and amount of consumables you need such as toner cartridges and paper. Choosing an MFD that is most appropriate for you is a complex decision given the wide range of models and combinations available. It's important to establish what functions—fax, printing, scanning, copying—are most important to you and find a machine that has strong specifications in those areas.

156. Share your office technology

Not every business can afford to purchase the wide array of office equipment needed to function effectively, let alone a multifunction device. However, with some organisation and planning the small business operator can reduce office technology costs by implementing some of the following strategies.

- Set up a network and share equipment with other staff. A friend of mine works in an office where three computers are linked to one printer and ten people share one fax machine.

- Share equipment with other businesses.

- How many computers do you really need? Can you share? When I managed a sales centre I always shared a computer with my office manager. I didn't need my own computer as I was always in the sales office supporting the sales consultants, speaking with customers and managing the team. If you do, be sure to have passwords and security devices installed.

157. Enter information just once

Modern technology is supposed to make your life easier, free up your time and save you money. It's important therefore to design your information processes so that the data you collect is only recorded once, at the time it is entered into the system. From here, it should be automatically accessible to other systems that need to track the same data.

Michael operates a direct marketing firm specialising in low-end consumer products. In the early days of his business he found he was doubling up on the amount of data entry to produce the reports he required to effectively manage his operations. When an order was received from a customer, the information was entered into a database system that produced a variety of reports. Unfortunately his old system did not have the capacity to produce certain essential documents so he had to re-enter much of the information into another program in order to develop the graphs, charts and spreadsheets required. For an $800 investment Michael upgraded his database software and he now enters the information only once. If he needs a report or graph, he just presses a few buttons and it prints out, saving him hundreds of hours and thousands of dollars a year.

158. Send birthday wishes over the Internet

If you can make the time to list your clients' birthdays and then send them a card every year, they will remember you fondly for a long time. I regularly receive birthday and Christmas cards from my gym, physiotherapist, dentist, work colleagues, clients and suppliers. While these cards are nice, they are usually quite plain, so try jazzing up your cards to create a positive impact on your customers. Send birthday cards to your friends, suppliers and customers over the Internet—e-cards are colourful, personal, interactive and fun, and the best news of all is they are free. There are a host of websites that provide a wide range of options for birthdays, congratulations cards, Christmas, Easter and so on.

159. Buy the same brand

There are excellent savings to be had from your business purchasing the same brand and model of equipment for each department. Firstly, you'll be able to get a better purchase price by buying in bulk from the same supplier. Secondly, the cost of buying consumables for the equipment will also be cheaper. Having the same brand also makes it a lot easier for your employees as they only need to learn how to operate one piece of equipment. A friend of mine once worked in a medium-sized investment firm that had five photocopiers, all individual makes and models. Each one operated differently with some being more complicated than others. Whenever my friend's regular photocopier broke down or became jammed, she would put off what she was doing until it was brought back to life.

Using the same brand also comes in handy if you are running short on consumables. One day my printer ran out of toner right in the middle of running off sales leads for my staff. I didn't have a spare cartridge on hand and it would have taken too long to order one from my supplier. It was also too expensive to buy toner from the local office supplies store so I just went next door to our administration office and pulled the toner cartridge out of their printer and put it in mine. When I had finished printing, I simply returned the cartridge to its original printer.

CHAPTER

8

TRAVEL

The world is continually becoming a smaller place in which to live. With increased competition and improved technology the cost of travel has decreased dramatically, but there are still many ways to keep your travel expenses to a minimum. This chapter demonstrates how to further reduce your travel overheads while maintaining an active travel schedule for your business.

HOTEL

Chapter 8

Travel

This chapter covers:

Managing your travel

Air fares

Hotels and accommodation

Travelling by car

Managing your travel

Gone are the days of the corporate junkets with large travel and expense accounts—or are they? In recent times, the collapse of major corporations has highlighted directors' blatant abuse and waste of corporate funds on first-class business travel and exorbitant entertainment expenses. These issues have been specifically singled out for much media attention and shareholder anger. There are very few businesses today, large or small, that can adequately justify the need for excessive expenditure on corporate travel and associated costs.

160. Do you really need to travel?

Travel is no longer the only option. Modern technology has evolved to the point where business travel can be dramatically reduced in exchange for a more cost-effective alternative. It is not uncommon to hear about people who have successfully conducted business with their clients for years without the two parties having ever met in person. A major challenge facing business owners is deciding whether an issue really needs to be dealt with in person or if the goal can be successfully achieved by implementing one, or a combination, of the following strategies.

Use the telephone

In many instances, a simple phone call can deal with most issues. Having had years of experience in the telemarketing industry, I can confidently say that the telephone is probably the most under-utilised of all business tools. I have solved everything over the phone, from payroll disputes and supply problems to customer complaints and threats of litigation.

Send an email

Email has revolutionised the way we do business. By using email you can communicate with large groups of people throughout the world. You can send reports, graphics, photographs, spreadsheets and a host of other documents over the Internet. Email is immediate, personal, convenient and secure, not to mention very cost-effective.

Post documents

Sometimes you just can't beat the good old-fashioned postal system. Many companies still conduct business wholly and solely by mail. In today's world where traditional letters are a rarity, a well-worded handwritten letter can produce a far greater effect than any form of electronic communication could ever have.

Use teleconferencing

A sales and marketing company I know holds quarterly teleconference calls between its eighteen regional managers. The calls last for just over an hour and are most productive. For this business, teleconferencing is a lot cheaper than flying everyone in for a meeting from all over Australia and New Zealand.

Delegate the responsibility

Does your company have a regional representative or manager who can attend to the issue at hand? For example, a major client has a problem with the level of service they are receiving from your sales reps. Do you drop everything to go and smooth things over personally or do you discuss the matter with your regional manager and get them to handle it? Delegate it to your manager—that's why you pay them big bucks in the first place, and they will appreciate your trust.

In most cases, you will probably use a combination of these strategies to achieve the desired result. If, however, travel is the only option, then go ahead and get yourself on the next available flight. Sometimes, you need to be there in person to show leadership or kick some butt.

161. Reduce the length of your trip

If you are travelling for business, aim to maximise the number of meetings, appointments, sales calls and site visits you can make. By simply planning ahead and preparing an itinerary, you can accomplish a great deal in the time allocated. Here are some suggestions to help you maximise the effectiveness of your business trips.

Travel time is not down time

Use your travelling time effectively by reviewing the strategies for your forthcoming appointments, writing thank you notes to send to some clients, reading a report, taking your 'in box' with you and attending to any overdue items, working on a new marketing strategy or developing an idea to save your business money.

Fill your time

Organise all appointments on the same day and try to keep them close to each other or even in the same place to cut travel costs and time. By being organised you can reduce the length of your trip, even if by only one day, saving your business money.

Seize the opportunity

Alternatively, look at extending your trip by one day to make the most of the opportunity.

Sherene flew to Singapore to attend a two-day retail trade fair. She extended her trip an extra day and visited a number of major shopping complexes on Orchard Road, having made prior arrangements with the Centre Management before leaving Australia. Sherene made the most of her trip to gain insights from one of the world's leading retail markets, and in doing so she avoided having to pay additional flight fares to return to Singapore.

Prepare for appointments

A week before the appointments, send out any relevant information, agendas or reports and reconfirm everything by email. This will allow everyone to be prepared and save a lot of time on the day. If you have local staff in the area, have them undertake any preparatory work that may be required.

Use stopover time effectively

If you are visiting more than one city on your business trip, try to schedule one of your meetings at the airport during a short stopover. Three or four hours to kill between flights can be put to good use by catching up with a client and buying them a meal at the airport, or meeting with your local area manager. This saves you money on taxi fares and uses your time efficiently.

162. Keep the number of people to a minimum

Bill is the national sales manager for a small but growing company dealing in home improvement products. A key to their growth has been the attendance at major home fairs and exhibitions around the country. For the first two events Bill was accompanied by his sales manager, Heather. He soon realised that his accommodation costs were going to double, as it was not appropriate for Heather and him to share the same hotel room. As a result, Bill reworked the itinerary for the seven remaining trade shows of the year so that he would now travel with another male manager and Heather would attend events with a female member of staff. There were also a number of smaller regional events that his company participated in. Bill and his team reviewed the effectiveness of these shows and decided to delete three of them from their marketing program. They also concluded that a single staff member could easily handle them on their own. These simple ideas saved Bill's business over $6000 in hotel accommodation in one year.

Take a leaf out of Bill's book and objectively rationalise how many people you need to send away on business trips. If more than one person is required, you need to be able to justify what that second person is going to do. And if two people are needed, try to structure it so that two males or two females travel at the same time so they can share a hotel room and cut accommodation costs in half.

163. Do a travel audit

One of the best ways to reduce your travel expenses is by having a look at exactly what your business is currently spending its travel budget on. Review your financial statements for the last couple of years and identify:

- the total amount spent on business-related travel

- a breakdown of expenses into travel, accommodation, entertainment and ancillary expenses

- the charges incurred for each category during each trip

- the total number of trips taken

- the reason why each trip occurred

- how many people were involved

- the length of each trip

- the outcomes of each trip—sales made, new clients established, problems solved.

This information will give you a comprehensive picture of how you spent your travel budget in the past. You can then determine whether any particular savings can be made through changing hotels for a cheaper alternative, cancelling certain trips, reducing the number of people going or using alternatives such as teleconferencing, email or a simple telephone call.

164. Develop a travel policy

A travel policy is essential in managing your travel expenses. If your employees are allowed to set their own limits on travel expenditure, you can expect some exorbitantly high reimbursement claims to reach your desk. Your travel policy should be fair to both your employees and your business. The Australian Taxation Office has published what is considered to be reasonable allowances for travel within Australia and internationally, covering items such as accommodation, meals and other expenses. Your business may choose to use this as a benchmark; however, I suggest that you should be flexible with allowances for overseas travel as those provided by the ATO cannot take into account fluctuations in the exchange rate. Your travel policy should clearly indicate what your business will pay for and up to what dollar amount. The policy should be given to all relevant employees prior to them undertaking any trip to ensure they are fully aware of what the company's obligations are.

165. Be flexible to save

Your company's negotiated corporate rate with a particular airline or hotel should not prevent you from taking advantage of cheaper options that provide a comparable service. The goal of any supply arrangement you enter into should be to provide you with the best possible product and service for the least amount of money. Your business should be flexible enough to take advantage of any potential saving opportunities that come your way.

Taryn's company markets hotel packages for five-star hotel chains, and one of the most frequent objections her sales staff come across is that a company already has an existing corporate arrangement with another hotel chain. On many occasions her staff are able to find out what these rates are and her packages are far cheaper—in some cases up to 40 per cent cheaper. Despite the obvious savings,

> *the prospect generally advises Taryn that it is company policy for all business accommodation to use an assigned corporate supplier. Whether through Taryn's packages or those of her competitors, these companies could save a huge amount of money on their corporate accommodation if they took a more flexible approach to booking procedures.*

166. Travel budget approval

Make it policy that all travel budgets require prior approval from an authorised manager prior to any travel arrangements being made. When I was working for a hotel chain in Malaysia, our sales manager regularly attended national and international trade shows and sales missions. All travel budgets had to be submitted to the director of sales and marketing for final approval. This simple step saved the company thousands of dollars. And once you've set the budget, stick to it.

167. Give sales people expense guidelines

Not having expense guidelines for your sales people is tantamount to giving them an open cheque book. Without any sort of limits your employees will tend to overspend while travelling and entertaining. Items such as telephone calls, rental cars and entertainment expenses should particularly be targeted. If the salesperson chooses to exceed these limits, they should pay the excess amount.

> *Tom operates a highly successful holiday sales centre and he told me about one of his managers who came to him with a $150 bar tab he had accumulated for entertaining the sales staff. Apart from sales being below par for the month, the manager had not sought Tom's approval prior to their little event. As no expense guidelines had actually been set, Tom decided to reimburse the manager for half of the bill and then hastily set about establishing a written guideline for entertainment expenses.*

You should also consider these two ideas when developing your expense guidelines.

Request receipts for everything

Regardless how minor the amount, you should demand receipts for anything an employee wishes to claim for reimbursement purposes. Many businesses set a minimum level of $10 as the base for which receipts must be provided. Employees often overestimate or round up small amounts on meals and incidentals that fall well under this limit.

Forgo travel advances

Do away with providing cash travel advances to employees. If employees have to pay with their own money first, most of them will think twice about overspending. This also reduces unnecessary administration costs and ensures the prompt submission of expense reports from employees on their return.

168. A leisurely approach

My wife and I spent a fantastic weekend at a beachfront resort for just over $100. That's only $50 a night—what a bargain! And it was made possible because of a promotion on the back of a shopping docket. There are literally hundreds of special deals, promotions and coupons that can provide you with fantastic travel savings. So why not use these deals for your corporate travel? Just because you are going on business doesn't mean you cannot take advantage of these excellent opportunities to save.

John owns an investment firm and travels and entertains extensively for business. He has two hotel memberships and uses the excellent accommodation rates they provide, including 50 per cent off rack rates plus half-price dining. He also subscribes to an entertainment booklet that offers him dining benefits at a wide range of restaurants. John is a frequent flyer member and once booked an accommodation deal in Melbourne that he saw advertised on a television travel and lifestyle program. Shopping dockets, coupons in the mail and special promotions in the newspapers have all added to the extensive savings John has made from his entertainment and travel program.

There's a saying that warns us never to mix business with pleasure. However, combining your business trip with a holiday can save you additional time away from your business, money for air fares, meals, transport and accommodation. My advice is to conduct any business first and then spend time afterwards enjoying your holiday. It's also worth checking with your accountant before you go to see what you will be able to claim as legitimate business expenses or tax deductions.

169. Travel as a reward

Rewarding staff for outstanding performance is crucial for all businesses to maintain high morale. A few years ago it became very trendy to use travel to popular local or international destinations as an incentive to high-performing employees. In many cases however, the cost of providing this reward extended further than just the costs of the holiday. Businesses incurred additional costs for the loss of staff time, increased payroll (to pay for relief staff) and administrative expenses.

When considering how to reward your high-performing employees, why not opt for a direct incentive that may cost only half the real value of the holiday but may be a bigger morale booster. Here are a few suggestions to get you started.

- Provide a monetary reward. A $1000 bonus may be more welcomed by your employee than a holiday that's costing you $2000. I know which I would choose!

- Pay for their car parking for a year.

- Give your employee an extra week of paid annual leave. Get them to take it during a quiet period so their absence will have minimal flow on effect.

170. Make all travel accountable

How many times have you sent employees away on business trips only to have them return with very little to show? Every trip, seminar, meeting, conference, trade show or sales mission must result in at least one great idea that is going to improve your sales, increase revenue, reduce costs, increase market share or put you ahead of the competition. Business trips that result in no tangible outcomes for your business are nothing more than a waste of money, no matter how hard you or your employees worked while away.

David regularly travels throughout Australia and South-East Asia, attending trade shows and sales missions to attract international students to local universities. Before he leaves, David meets with his director to set out specific goals for each event. On his return David produces a report providing detailed information on which goals were achieved and how, along with justifications as to why specific goals were not met. The report includes information such as who he met and the outcome of the meeting, any new business that was confirmed, any potential new business for follow-up within the next three, six or twelve months, other potential business opportunities, any promotion and marketing opportunities that were identified, relevant information on their competitors and any new market trends. The information in this report is then used to update the company's sales and marketing strategies and adjust their business practices as they see fit.

Air fares

Regardless of whether you fly first class, business class or cattle class, air fares cost your business money. However, air travel is crucial to the success of many businesses and the following are good tips to keep your air fare expenses to a minimum while still enabling you to run your business effectively.

171. Use the Internet

Book tickets on-line and save yourself a great deal of time and money. The Internet is very efficient as your booking is confirmed immediately and can be done from the convenience of your home or office. While on-line you can also check the best and cheapest times and days for travelling and make your bookings accordingly so that you get the best deal. I have found that booking my domestic travel over the Internet also saves between $10 and $20 a ticket, compared to booking the same fare through a travel agent. Be aware, however, that Internet fares tend to be very restrictive, so ensure the dates you booked are not going to change. Most airlines have a non-refundable policy regardless of how early you cancel the flight; however, some do provide you with a credit for the amount of your ticket (minus a small cancellation fee) which can be used for other bookings with the same carrier.

172. Frequent flyer savings

If you do a lot of travelling in your business, make sure you enrol in frequent flyer programs offered by airline and credit card companies. While many people lost enormous amounts of frequent flyer points with the sudden collapse of Ansett airline, these programs still provide a great deal of value. Apart from flying mileage, frequent flyer points can also be accumulated through affiliated credit card programs whereby every time you spend one dollar on your credit card your earn a set amount of frequent flyer points. If you have such a credit card, you would be wise to use it for as many purchases as possible and earn more points. Be sure to always pay off your monthly minimum balance on these cards as they often charge interest rates that are higher than normal.

173. First-class travel means a first-class price tag

I can never understand how a business justifies paying for business or first-class air fares for their staff, especially on short-haul journeys. Most airlines have worked hard to make economy class as comfortable as possible. The potential savings on a one-hour journey can run to more than $200 each way—multiply that by the number of flights in a year and the potential savings for a company can be tens of thousands of dollars. If you must fly business class, then use those frequent flyer points to get a free upgrade.

The introduction of Virgin Blue into the Australian market has seen them pick up a large share of the cost-conscious business traveller market.

On one Virgin flight from Sydney to Brisbane I sat next to a gentleman called Leigh who owns a national company providing interior fittings for hotels and serviced apartments. We got talking and discovered that we both had a mutual friend working in the hotel industry. I later spoke to our friend and discovered that Leigh's small company is the market leader in his industry and turns over millions of dollars a year in business. I asked Leigh why he wasn't flying in the grand comfort of business class on another airline and he was very quick to inform me that his company didn't get to where it is today by wasting money on extravagances such as business class travel, especially on a trip where the journey is so short.

Most small business people no longer expect hot face towels and free meals—airline food was never very good anyway. They would rather save their money for other more profitable things like entertaining a client.

174. Be flexible with your travel times

Considerable savings can be made on your business travel if you are prepared to be flexible with your departure and arrival times, by travelling on the lowest traffic days and during the lowest traffic times of the day. Midweek and Saturdays are often the best days to travel; during the middle of the day are the best times to get reduced fares. Peak travel times are usually 7 am to 9 am and 4 pm to 7 pm. I recently booked an air fare from Sydney to Melbourne departing after 10.30 am for only $180 return. If I had chosen to leave two hours earlier, I would have paid around $280. I was able to save $100 on just one trip by being flexible with my travel schedule.

In some cases, staying overnight may actually mean you will save substantially on your ticket price. So if you are in no hurry to get to your final destination, the cost of your accommodation doesn't outweigh the savings made and you are able to use your stopover wisely—you could make some cold sales calls, check out the competition or meet with a client—it may well be worth your while.

Try to avoid any travel around busy holiday periods in both your country of departure and of arrival. Not only are air fares much more expensive during these periods, it is also very difficult to use your frequent flyer points as blockout dates are enforced. I was thinking of combining a business trip and personal holiday to Malaysia at the end of the year until my travel agent advised the air fare would be $4000 for a return ticket. This was three times more expensive than a normal fare and I was giving plenty of notice by booking six months in advance. It turned out that three key holiday festivals were all occurring at approximately the same time, resulting in a huge demand for tickets from expatriate Malaysians wishing to return home for the holidays.

If you can be really flexible with your travel times, consider purchasing an Advanced Purchase Excursion (APEX) fare. You are normally required to purchase these tickets 21 days in advance for international flights and 14 days for domestic flights. As these fares are waitlisted, you may have to spend considerable time hanging around the airport waiting for the next available flight.

175. Check your booking

Be sure to confirm all the details of your trip before purchasing the ticket. When booking through a travel agent ensure they fax or email a copy of your itinerary to you. This will avoid costly ticket changes that eat up any savings you may have made on your ticket price, not to mention the dramas at the airport when you finally realise the details are wrong. This almost happened to me when I was flying from Kuala Lumpur to Singapore for a trade show. After booking the flight with a travel agent, I requested a faxed itinerary; I immediately checked it and noticed there was a mistake with the departure dates. If I hadn't confirmed the details I would have discovered on arrival at the airport that my confirmed flight had actually left 24 hours earlier—without me on it.

176. Save on travel insurance

If you are doing a lot of travelling, particularly internationally, consider the benefits of taking out travel insurance. Travel insurance will save you a great deal of money in the event of anything going wrong either with your luggage, your travel plans or you! However, before you purchase separate travel insurance, investigate the following options.

Credit cards

Many credit card companies provide comprehensive travel insurance cover if you purchase your plane tickets using their credit cards. My card provides this service and I use it every time I travel.

Bank accounts

Keep an eye out for offers made by many of the banks. As part of a certain savings plan or account, the banks sometimes include free insurance coverage when you go on holiday.

Private health funds

If you have private health insurance, check the policy thoroughly and you may find that it also provides travel insurance cover.

Other insurance and superannuation policies

If you have other insurance or superannuation policies, contact the policy provider and see if they offer free or discounted travel insurance as part of their plan. If they don't already, they may consider introducing it in the future.

Corporate insurance plan

Companies with a large number of staff who travel internationally often open a corporate or group travel insurance policy. If this is relevant to you, speak with your insurer and see if they can add this benefit onto an existing policy your company has with them for a small increase in your premiums.

Hotels and accommodation

Whether you want to go five-star or just find a place where you can sleep for the night, accommodation is a necessity for most business travel. Whatever your preference, these suggestions will help you save money on business accommodation.

177. Stay with friends or relatives

Why not save money on your accommodation by staying with friends or relatives. I know my family would *expect* me to stay with them if I was travelling to my hometown on business. While this sounds like a great idea—and it is—there are some ground rules that need to be observed to ensure friendly and hospitable relations between host and guest are maintained well after you have left.

■ Make sure the house or apartment is big enough for everyone; two friends stayed with my wife and me for a couple of days in our one-bedroom apartment. The next time one of them came to town they preferred to rent a cheap hotel room—enough said!

■ The arrangement is reciprocal, so be prepared to offer the same hospitality should your hosts come to your city.

■ You don't have to do it all the time—if you are travelling regularly to one destination then don't make a habit of always staying with the same people. There's nothing worse than stretching the friendship.

■ Buy your hosts a gift or take them out to dinner. It's a small price to pay compared to the cost of a couple of nights in a hotel.

178. A few tricks of the trade when booking hotel accommodation

If you are making your own hotel reservations, ensure that you are getting the best available deal.

Call the hotel direct

When making hotel reservations talk directly to the hotel staff rather than using the 1800 central reservation line, and ask for their best rate. Often, hotels have special discounts and promotions on offer that may not be as well promoted through the central reservations centre.

Request a standard room

Ask the reservation staff for the price of a standard room. This is the lowest category of room and more than sufficient if you will be spending little time in it. Often they will quote on a higher category of room in an attempt to upsell a guest. Although the rate might still be attractive, the standard room will always be the cheapest option.

Seek frequent usage discounts

If you are doing a lot of travelling, seek out hotel chains that have properties in as many of the locations you travel to and negotiate rates below the corporate standard. Depending on your usage you may be able to get further discounts of 5 to 30 per cent below the corporate rate.

Inquire at check-in

Even if your accommodation rate has been booked, always inquire upon check-in if there is a cheaper or better value rate. Different rates, new promotions and special packages may have been released between the time you made your booking and your arrival. This could definitely be the case if you always book well in advance.

Select hotels based on location to save costs

Save on taxi fares, car rental costs and time by choosing a hotel close to where the majority of your meetings are being held. The extra $10 per night you pay for the hotel will be quickly offset by the $20 taxi fare you save in having to get to your appointments.

Use the Internet

There are a plethora of hotel reservation sites on the web. Use them and put the popular ones in your Favourites menu. Review the conditions of use, particularly arrival times and cancellation fees.

179. Some things to consider during your stay

Now that you've got yourself a decent hotel for a good rate, don't waste any savings you have so gained so far. There are a number of traps that can quickly add up to huge expenses—I know, I literally lived in a hotel for twelve months.

Notify of cancellation

If you are going to be delayed or aren't going to make it at all, then ensure you notify the hotel prior to your arrival. Most hotels require cancellation at least 24 hours prior to your due check-in time to avoid any penalties. Ask for a cancellation number and write it down in your diary along with the name of the reservation staff. No business can afford to pay for hotel accommodation that they have not used.

Skip heavy hotel surcharges

Rather than get stuck with high surcharges for local and long-distance calls from your hotel room, use the public phone in the hotel lobby. Many hotels put a 100 per cent surcharge on calls made from their rooms. When travelling abroad, use toll-free access numbers or get an international calling card.

Avoid using room service

If you must eat in the hotel, go down to the restaurant rather than order room service. The hotel places a hefty surcharge on room service meals and it isn't uncommon to pay $15 for a hamburger and chips. Numerous restaurants, cafes and other cheaper dining alternatives surround most hotels.

Stay clear of the minibar

Unless you think it's reasonable to pay $5 for a can of coke, $3 for a Mars bar and $8 for a can of beer, then steer well clear of the mini bar in your room. If you are staying for a couple of days, take a walk to the nearest convenience store and stock up on supplies.

Always check your bill

Don't take it for granted that your bill is correct. I have often received extra charges on my hotel bill for services I never used. Dispute any items that should not be on your bill before you leave the hotel as it's much easier to do so before you've forked out the cash.

Take advantage of hotel courtesies

Take advantage of the freebies provided by the hotel during your stay. These could include complimentary welcome drink, free use of the fitness centre, toiletries, breakfasts and free courtesy bus to and from the airport.

Travelling by car

Whether you need to get around while away on business or just get around during the course of your day, the humble motor car can cost you and your business both time and money.

180. Car rental savings

If you must hire a car while travelling on business, consider the following ideas to keep costs to a minimum.

Use smaller cars

Reserve a small or midsize vehicle, as these are much cheaper and generally more fuel-efficient. When picking up your car ask for a free upgrade.

Do a thorough inspection

Be sure to check the car for any scratches, dents or marks and note them on the inspection form before departing. If these are not identified you could be liable for any repairs regardless of whether they were your fault.

Skip car rental insurance

You may be able to waive the collision and liability insurance on car rentals after checking your regular auto insurance policy. Some policies provide coverage when using rental vehicles. If you have taken out travel insurance, this may also cover rental cars.

Fill up the tank

Make it a point to fill up the petrol tank before returning the car to the rental company to avoid hefty charges for a partially full tank.

Return the car on time

Have the car returned to the rental company before the due deadline, otherwise you may be liable for an extra day's rental.

181. Use alternatives to car rental

Unless you plan to do a lot of driving while away on your business trip, renting a car may become more expensive than one of these cheaper options.

- Many hotels provide free or cheap shuttle buses and courtesy vans and limousines. Check to see if these services are available and how much they cost when making your reservation.

- If you only need to travel between the airport and the hotel, consider catching a train or bus to your hotel.

- Using taxis or public transport to get to meetings can be more cost-effective as you do not have to worry about parking and petrol costs along with the car rental cost, nor do you need to find your way around in a strange city and locate parking. There are also added costs when driving in some countries; for example, London has recently introduced a toll for all cars driving into the city centre, and many countries have road tolls which are expensive when converted to Australian dollars.

- Do you have family or friends who can drive you to and from the airport?

- You may find that a client or company representative will pick you up from the airport.

CHAPTER 9

INVENTORY CONTROL

The products your business sells are the backbone of your operation, for without them there would be no business. Businesses struggle on a daily basis to have enough stock to meet the demands of their customers without having too much just sitting on the shelf. There are substantial cost savings to be made for every business that manages their inventory well. This chapter will help you get your money out of storage and back in your pocket where it belongs.

Chapter 9

Inventory control

This chapter covers:

182. Know when to order your products

One of the simplest ways to reduce your inventory expenses and the associated storage costs is to determine the best time to order new or replacement stock. As inventory levels fall, you must know at what point a new order should be placed to ensure you are still able to meet the demands of your customers. This point is often known as the order (or reorder) point. When you reach the designated order point, it is time to immediately request more stock from your supplier.

Knowing when is the right time to reorder stock is crucial for Jim's sports goods store. 'There is nothing worse than a sale walking out the door because you haven't got their size, colour or design in stock,' he explains. Much of his business is seasonal and so the stock levels of the different items go up and down in accordance with what sports are being played at the time. It only takes 24 hours at the most for Jim to receive a new supply of footballs or basketballs, so he sets a reorder point of two for these items; when there are only two basketballs left on the shelf, he places another order. However, during the heart of the basketball season he increases his reorder point to five as there is a much higher demand for the product.

Determining your order point will differ from business to business; however, there are some common factors that all businesses will need to take into consideration.

- How much of the stock is sold or used on a daily, weekly or fortnightly basis?

- How long does it take for your supplier to deliver the products?

- Are there any savings to be gained from increasing or decreasing your order point?

- Are there any seasonal factors that may affect your order point?

183. Don't keep any stock reserves at all

Many companies, particularly those in the manufacturing sector, have moved towards a leaner and more efficient system of production that requires literally no storage of raw materials. The just-in-time (JIT) system, as its name suggests, is a method where all the raw materials and parts needed at each stage of production are brought together at the exact time they are required. As a direct result the manufacturer has no inventory or storage costs other than the supply of the raw products.

Many small businesses actually start out using the just-in-time system without even realising it, then as their business expands and the orders start to pile in they change focus and begin to mass-produce their products.

Adam was a budding entrepreneur who regularly attended garage sales, flea markets and antique fairs, successfully buying and selling odds and ends for a healthy profit. As he was very good at what he did, he decided to produce a booklet on how to make money from other people's junk. He marketed it through direct mail letters, adverts in the classified section of local papers and by handing out flyers at different events around town. To keep his costs to a minimum, Adam would wait until an order was received then print a copy of the booklet from his PC and take it to the printer for binding. On many occasions he provided plastic binders and clear plastic covers that he had recycled from reports thrown out at work. As the demand for his booklet increased, Adam decided to have 200 copies printed at a copying centre as his personal printer couldn't cope with producing that many copies at once. He soon discovered his profit margins and cash reserves had dropped significantly as a result. While confident he would sell all the publications, he had increased his expenses and storage requirements. Plus, the money tied up in printed booklets could have been sitting in his bank earning him interest.

184. What to do when you have excess inventory

You suddenly find yourself in a situation where you have more stock on hand than you can deal with. The product has been sitting on your display shelves for months, there are still boxes of the stuff clogging up your storeroom and you can think of ten better things you could be doing with all the cash you've used to buy the goods in the first place. What do you do?

Spiro runs a liquor store in the suburbs and has a very philosophical attitude towards having too much stock. 'It happens sometimes. No matter how much planning I do and how careful I am, once in a while I'm left holding half a dozen cases of wine or spirits that just won't move. That's business! There's no use complaining about it because it will still be there the next day when I come in. I just make the decision to get rid of it as quickly as possible.' Spiro explains that achieving a big profit margin is not a consideration when trying to clear excess inventory. He is more concerned about clearing space for more profitable products and recovering his initial costs. If he can make a small profit at the same time, then that is a bonus.

Here are a few ideas that have worked well for Spiro and many other businesses who have found themselves with a little too much inventory to sell.

Have a sale

It's an oldie but still a goodie! Can you reduce the selling price and have a special sale for that particular item? The key to moving items quickly is the price, so don't just give a 15 per cent discount—cut your losses and cut the price. Once you've made a decision to get rid of it, make sure you merchandise it well. Place a display right by the front door or cash register with a big sign showing the savings.

Package with another product

Can you combine the outstanding stock with another product and offer them as a special deal?

Spiro once found himself with two dozen extra corkscrews that he had hoped to sell for Father's Day. Unfortunately, the items were not as popular as he had hoped. The retail price of the item was $29.95, though the actual cost to Spiro was only $5.00. He decided to package the corkscrew with two bottles of wine, a white and a red, and sell them off as a promotion. Customers could purchase two bottles of wine for $30 and receive a fantastic corkscrew, valued at the same amount, for free. Five days later there were no more corkscrews left. Problem solved.

Get your staff to promote it

Every customer who enters your business should be made aware of the promotion you are running to get rid of excess stock. When they come to the cash register to pay for their purchases, have your staff say something like,

'Have you heard about the great promotion we're running at the moment? Simply buy these two bottles of delicious XYZ wine and you'll receive this fantastic corkscrew, valued at $29.95, for free.' It doesn't hurt to ask—the customer can only say no to the promotion, but they might also say yes.

Location, location, location

Can you relocate the product to a more visual part of your business? Sometimes just placing items in a more visible spot stimulates sales. You could place them on a display stand outside the front door, near the cash register, inside the main entrance, at the front end of an aisle or next to a high-selling product.

Offer to existing customers

Do you have an up-to-date customer database? Why not offer the stock to existing customers at a special rate? Set a short time frame for the offer in order to create some urgency, and be sure to say that this offer is exclusive to them because they are loyal customers. Though not making a large profit, you will be disposing of the dead inventory and creating further goodwill with your customers, which can only be a good thing for your business.

Return to supplier

See if you can give the stock back to the supplier in return for a credit note that you can use to purchase other products from them. If the items are not perishable, you should be able to do some sort of deal with your supplier.

Jim had bought some sports equipment from the manufacturer but it didn't sell anywhere near as well as he had hoped. Although the items were not bought on consignment, Jim went back to the manufacturer and was able to negotiate a credit for the returned goods. The manufacturer was happy to help as Jim was a regular customer and they would be able sell the goods to another customer.

Throw it away

In some cases you may not be able to sell that product so the garbage bin may be the only place for it. This is certainly the case with perishable goods that have a specific shelf life. If this is the only option available, consult your accountant first as you may be able claim it as a tax write-off. Alternatively, if you simply can't sell then give it away. Donate the goods to a charity or community organisation. You won't get any money for it but you could get some excellent free publicity for your good deed.

Sometimes, having excess inventory is not just the result of bad planning or management. Environmental factors such as a sudden drop in the economy or bad publicity about a particular industry could also leave you overstocked. As my friend Spiro says, 'It's not what's happened which is important, it's what you decide to do about it'.

185. Keep your stock to a minimum

As Spiro said, sometimes no matter what you do, you will end up with too much inventory on your hands. The good news is there are some simple strategies you can put in place to reduce the possibility of being caught out again. Can you implement any of the following in your business?

- Don't increase your order size just because the supplier offers you a discount for a bigger purchase. It's pointless buying an additional 200 widgets with 15 per cent discount if they are going to sit on the shelf and in the storeroom for the next twelve months.

- Don't simply go through the motions of ordering more stock just because the salesman has arrived. Erwin suddenly realised after four months that they had far too many water containers for the office water cooler. Every two weeks the supplier would automatically replace the empty containers, even though there were twice that number of full containers in stock.

- Don't be pressured into ordering more than you need by the sales representative. That is why they are called *sales* reps because their job is to sell as much of everything as they possibly can. If you don't need an item, tell the rep it's not required—they can't force you to buy!

- Does your business have more than one location where stock is kept? If so you could be duplicating your inventory.

- Seek out suppliers that are prepared to provide stock on a consignment basis. This is where you only pay for what you sell and the remaining items can be returned to the supplier at no cost to yourself.

- Is it possible for the supplier to make more than one delivery a week without any extra charge? Regular deliveries mean you can order less stock each time and hence use less storage space.

■ Can you reduce the number of items you stock? The 80/20 principle would apply in most businesses where 80 per cent of sales come from only 20 per cent of the items being sold. So it's important to track the items that sell and those that don't and dispose of the non-performing products.

186. What happens when the stock does run out?

Keeping your inventory to a minimum means you have to accept there will be occasions when stock runs out. By anticipating this may happen, you can prepare some counterstrategies to ensure your lack of stock doesn't necessarily result in a lost sale.

Get from another location

If you have more than one outlet, utilise your network to its fullest extent to fill the customer's order. For example, it is common for clothing and shoe shops to contact other branches when a colour or size is unavailable, and even to arrange prompt delivery to the store rather than have the customer go out of their way.

Upsell, cross-sell

Not having the exact product the customer wants doesn't mean losing the sale. Explore other options with them and you will be surprised how many take you up on your suggestions.

A friend recently told me that a large office equipment supplier was selling combination phone/fax/answering machine systems for a real bargain. I dropped in to their store early on a Saturday morning but was informed that they had sold the last of the stock just ten minutes ago. The employee then asked whether it was that particular model I was interested in; I told her it was the low price rather than the brand that had attracted me. She proceeded to show me a number of similar models they had in stock and within fifteen minutes had sold me one that cost $70 more than what I was initially going to pay, but it was a well-known brand and I was happy with the price.

Get from a non-competing store

Barry has run a pool maintenance and supplies store for the past fifteen years, and in that time has built up a list of very loyal clients. One such customer came to order some chemicals for his pool. Business had been particularly brisk that day and Barry had unexpectedly run out of stock. Not wanting to disappoint a loyal customer, Barry had the gentleman pay for his order and told him he would deliver the goods to the customer's home within forty-five minutes. While his assistant looked after the store, Barry drove to a nearby pool supplies store two suburbs away, paid for the products with the customer's cash (receiving a 10 per cent trade discount off the retail price) and then drove to the customer's house to deliver the goods. Although he had run out of stock and only made a 10 per cent profit on the goods sold, it was still a small profit and more importantly Barry had kept that customer's business.

187. Expect your suppliers to perform on time, every time

Your ability to service your customers' needs is greatly dependent on the ability of your suppliers to deliver the right products in the right amounts at the right time. Suppliers' failure to live up to these expectations can cause you to lose business, as the following case illustrates.

Angela and her partner went to dine at a small restaurant by the beach on the recommendation of a colleague who had been there the previous weekend. It was over thirty minutes drive away; however, her colleague had talked nonstop about how beautiful the views were and how delicious the seafood platter was. The views certainly were spectacular, but Angela and her partner were extremely disappointed when they were told that due to a delivery delay the famous seafood platter was not available. Many others in the restaurant were also disappointed and Angela noticed a number of people get up and leave as soon as they heard the restaurant's signature dish was unavailable. The following week at work Angela informed her colleagues of their disappointment. Two others from her office had been planning to go to the restaurant with their husbands on the coming weekend, but decided to go elsewhere after hearing Angela's experience.

Make it clear to your suppliers that you expect outstanding service from them. And when their level of service falters, hold the supplier accountable for correcting the problem. If one of your suppliers consistently underperforms, it would be wise to look for another company to take their place. Your livelihood depends on it.

188. Control access to supplies and inventory

It's an unfortunate fact but employee pilferage does take place. It's important to control the number of people who have access to supplies and inventory, so put supplies in a locked cabinet or room and limit the number of people with access to them. It's not a matter of distrusting your employees as much as a matter of employees being careless with supplies if they have unlimited access to them. In terms of inventory, it's just as important to limit access to your warehouse or storeroom and make sure all items are checked out and checked back in again. Only those responsible for managing the inventory should have access to stock. Make it a strict policy that other employees must be accompanied by an authorised person to access inventory storage areas.

189. Reduce office storage requirements

It's amazing how many useless documents and correspondence we can accumulate in the space of a few short months, let alone a couple of years. Does your business have a hoarding mentality where five different people keep a copy of every single piece of paper? The fewer documents you keep, the less money you need to spend on filing cabinets, manila folders and the like. This could also mean you might not require as large an office or so much storage space.

Allan is an old friend and a very successful businessman. He can't stand having too much stuff lying around his office, so every six months he and his employees spend half a day having a spring clean-out. Allan has his employees ask themselves, 'Do I really need to keep this?' and 'What is the worst possible thing that could happen if I throw this out?' If their answer does not put them or the company in prison, get them or the company in trouble with government authorities, lose the company customers or affect efficiency, then he encourages them to get rid of it. To further encourage frugal record-keeping, Allan has instituted a filing cabinet policy for the whole office. Each member of staff is only allowed one three-drawer filing cabinet in which to store all their work, with some exceptions depending on their role.

190. Check your inventory on delivery

Do you or your employees physically check the quantity and quality of supplies as soon as they are delivered? If you don't then you should. It is a lot easier to get damaged goods replaced if they are spotted at the time of delivery rather than two or three days later. You should check for the following.

■ Are the goods the exact model, type and make that you ordered?

■ Has the correct quantity been delivered?

■ Are any of the goods damaged or are there any defects?

Most people dislike having their name spelt incorrectly. For this reason Emma, the membership manager for a national business organisation, ensures the membership cards she receives from her supplier are checked on delivery. An employee cross-references customers' names on the list that was sent to the supplier against the names embossed on each membership card. Prior to employing this system, her company had lost a number of customers because of names spelt incorrectly on personalised membership cards. Now if a name is identified as having been spelt incorrectly, the correct details are faxed to the supplier who rectifies the mistake and sends out the replacement card at no cost to Emma.

Knowing what to look for is only half the battle. You must also have a system in place that will enable your employees to complete an inventory check in the most efficient and effective manner. The following strategies will assist you to do just that.

■ Delegate the responsibility of checking all inventory to one or two people.

- Provide them with adequate training so they can clearly identify damaged goods.

- Demonstrate the process required if goods are damaged or the order is incorrect.

- Have them keep accurate records of all inventory received.

- Ensure all goods received are checked against the original purchase order or invoice.

Through effectively managing the delivery of your inventory, you can control any potential loss or waste resulting from incorrect orders.

191. Opportunity cost

And if you needed any more convincing of the benefits of keeping inventory levels to a minimum, just consider what you could be doing with all that extra money tied up in product that is sitting on your shelves or your storeroom floor:

- investing in marketing strategies

- conducting research

- purchasing new technology to save you time and money

- keeping it in the bank earning interest

- investing in stocks and shares.

CHAPTER

10

GETTING PAID AND PAYING THE BILLS

Cash is king for any small business. The flow of cash in and out of your business constitutes its lifeblood. Unfortunately, getting paid can sometimes be a costly exercise. This chapter shows you how to get paid on time—or even early—without additional cost to your business. You will also learn how to manage your payments to ensure they work to your best possible advantage.

Chapter 10

Getting paid and paying the bills

This chapter covers:

Getting paid

Paying the bills

Getting paid

Just getting paid for the goods and services you provide can cost your business a small fortune. Unpaid accounts, the time and energy spent on chasing up late payments, the cost of collection agencies and legal bills can all be a huge drain on your resources. Prevention is always better than cure so avoid putting yourself in a position where you are owed money. These tips will help you do just that.

192. Give your customers different payment options

Make it easier to get your money from your customers by making it easier for them to pay you. By offering a variety of different options to your customers, you are more likely to get payment up-front. Here are a few examples to consider.

Credit cards

If your business does not accept credit cards, you don't know what you are missing out on. Yes, there are fees and charges attached to all credit card transactions, but these can be renegotiated with the banks. The sheer convenience of credit cards for both the customer and your business should be more than enough reason to accept them.

EFTPOS

Like credit cards, EFTPOS provides convenience and reduces the amount of cash kept on the premises.

Direct debit

One of the greatest things to ever happen to the fitness industry was the monthly debiting of membership fees from members' credit cards. Members sign up for a full twelve months and the monthly membership fee is debited. This simple process has increased the profitability of fitness centres by ensuring regular payments are received at a minimal administrative cost. Renewal of memberships after the initial twelve months has also increased dramatically because the money is continually deducted until the member cancels the membership. Because the amount is minimal, many people just accept it and keep their membership alive.

Lay-by/hire-purchase

Most department stores and other retail outlets do it with great success. Can you offer lay-by for any of your products?

Cash

Believe it or not, I was recently informed by a salesperson that 'we do not accept cash payments'. I couldn't believe what I was hearing! I just put my money back in my pocket and walked out the door.

Cheque/money order

If you accept cheque payments, just be sure that you do not release the product to the customer until the cheque has been cleared by the bank and the money is sitting in your account.

Direct deposit

Many direct mail, Internet and direct marketing companies are finding an increased demand from their customers to pay for products by depositing cash directly into the supplier's bank account. My wife and I regularly use this payment method to purchase items from Internet shopping sites such as eBay.

Internet transfer

I have one particular client who insists on paying me via a bank transfer over the Internet. Once the transfer has been made, he emails me and I log on to my bank account and check the deposit has been successful. It's as easy as that.

Obviously some methods are better than others and it really does depend on the type of business you are running and the cost of purchases customers make from you. However, when choosing the best methods for your business, also consider the opportunity costs involved. I know a number of small business operators who accept credit card payments despite the $20 per month account charge plus merchant fees for each transaction. Many of them believe this is a small price to pay to know they have the money in the bank and don't have to spend extra time and resources chasing up overdue accounts.

193. Insist on prompt payment

Taking a long time to collect money owed to you can be a major cost to your business. Small business operators cannot afford to have a conscience when it comes to collecting payment for goods sold or services offered. Set your payment terms and stick to them religiously. Insist your customers provide prompt payment in accordance with these terms, as you will naturally have a number of customers that will stretch payment as long as possible past the due-by date. If they do then you need to be prepared to act accordingly in order to get your money.

The day after their payment term has expired, telephone every customer with outstanding bills. In many cases, the reasons for non-payment are quite innocent. Your invoice may have gone astray or the person responsible for authorising payment of the invoice has gone on holiday for three weeks and the bill is sitting in their in-tray. In my experience the longer you put it off, the harder it is to get your payment, so keep calling them every day until the bill is paid. This also sends a very clear message to customers that you will not accept late payment. Remember, your payment terms are just that—*your* terms, not your customers'. You set the standards that they must follow and not the other way around.

194. Accept part payments—as a last resort

If your customers are experiencing tough times and finding it difficult to pay you the full amount in one go, you may wish to consider offering them a payment plan whereby they pay you a lesser amount over a set period of time until the full amount is paid. You may also decide to include a penalty charge on top of the original amount to cover any additional administration expenses.

Shane was owed $2400 by a customer who purchased computer software from his business. The customer was a regular client of two years and had a good history of paying on time with only a few short delays. A fortnight after the payment was due, Shane met with his customer to discuss the outstanding bill. His client informed him that their business had recently suffered a major setback through the loss of four major accounts to a colleague who had left to start up his own operation. As things were slow he was not in a position to meet the full amount in one payment. Not wanting to walk out empty-handed *and fearing the hassles associated with chasing up outstanding accounts, Shane suggested a part payment plan to the client whereby they would pay $300 every month until the account was paid, along with a penalty charge of $250. Should the outstanding bill be paid in full prior to the fifth month, the penalty charge would be waived.*

When entering into any sort of agreement as outlined above, don't forget to write up a short contract stating payment terms and conditions and get both parties to sign it. Remember, a solid cash flow is the number one goal of your business, so any cash coming in is better than none.

195. Don't offer credit at all

In my opinion, the best way to avoid any problems getting your money is by asking for payment up-front. When I first started selling my self-published manuals, I was so ecstatic seeing the orders rolling in that I would send out a copy to the customer along with an invoice for payment. My payment terms were 30 days, but I anticipated this wouldn't be required as the customer would send me a cheque straight away. How wrong I was! After the first three months I was already owed $500; this represented a significant number of bad debtors for a product that cost less than $20. I decided to take a stand: it's now money up-front or no deal. A purchase order without payment is only an inquiry, not an order. By shifting my customers to this payment method, I have also reduced administration by half and I no longer have any problems with collection costs.

As business operators, there are a number of key factors we need to understand in order to successfully implement an up-front payment system.

- Take a stand. You need to set the policy in writing, inform all staff and customers and stick to it.

- How unique are you? If your customers can't get the product or service you are offering elsewhere, they have no option other than to do business with you on your terms.

- Let it be your competitors' problem. Many businesses are worried that customers will go to their competitors who do offer extended payment terms and credit facilities. This may be the case, but your competitors will also suffer all the added costs and stress associated with chasing up overdue payments.

- Provide quality. Keep your customers from going elsewhere by providing a quality product and outstanding service.

- Maximise opportunity costs. Use the time and resources you have saved by not having to deal with bad debtors, to proactively seek out new business.

196. If you must offer credit, cover yourself

If your business offers credit terms to customers, you are in effect lending them your own money—now that's a thought to make any business operator take note. Nevertheless, if you do offer credit, here are some strategies to increase your chances of being paid on time and to reduce the amount of time, effort and money you may have to spend in getting your own money back.

Screen customers thoroughly

How carefully are your customers screened? All customers, regardless of how well you know them, should complete a thorough credit application with a minimum of three credit references. Make sure you check the references: just because a customer has written down the names of three well-known companies as credit references, doesn't mean to say they have actually ever done business with them before. As part of the screening process, check out a customer's credit rating through personal credit reports on the business's owner, letters of credit and financial statements.

Offer credit on a case-by-case basis

Don't jump in headfirst and offer every customer the same credit terms. Not every customer deserves the same arrangements, so you are best advised to assess credit on an individual company basis. Consider elements such as how long they have been doing business with you, the amount of credit required and alternative payment options.

How long have they been in business?

Before extending any credit find out how long the business has been operating. If they have been around for more than five years, they are more likely to pay their bills on time or they wouldn't still exist.

Reduce your billing terms

Can you reduce the length of your billing period so you get paid sooner? For example, reduce 30-day payment terms to 21- or even 14-day periods. This will have a dramatic effect on your cash flow.

Be flexible sometimes

If a good customer is occasionally late with payment, be flexible. Sometimes customers get themselves in a short-term financial pinch and are being truthful when they tell you they will pay the amount owed once the problems are cleared up. Do continue to call them to request payment, and set up a payment plan if necessary. Resort to extended payments only in emergencies.

197. Sometimes no is the right answer

You have researched a company's credit history and are still not totally confident about extending their credit. The answer is simple: don't do it! The potential loss of business (if they do go elsewhere) is offset by the problems and added expense of having a customer that doesn't pay their bills. A slow-paying customer can sometimes be far worse than no customer at all. Once you factor in the time and energy you spend tracking and collecting their outstanding invoices, these delinquent customers may in fact be costing you more money than they're worth. So get rid of the dead weight and spend your time and money looking for better paying customers. I don't know of any business anywhere in the world that went bust because they declined an application for credit from a customer—but we probably all know of businesses that have collapsed because of so many bad debts from unpaid bills.

198. Don't let invoicing back up

Cash is the lifeblood of your business and letting your billing slide for any reason can have terminal consequences. No business can justify not billing customers as soon as possible after the order is placed or the service is performed. Unfortunately, just sending out an invoice doesn't necessarily guarantee you will get paid on time or at all. The good news is you can increase your chances of being paid by implementing the following simple strategies.

Send invoices immediately

If you are not getting invoices out straight away, it will prove very costly to your business. Look at your current invoicing system and see if any improvements can be made to ensure an invoice is sent out the same day the order is received. If you provide goods on credit, send your invoices with the product, rather than separately in the mail. Not only will the customer receive the invoice immediately, you will save on postal costs.

Make invoices accurate

Billing mistakes can cost your business thousands of dollars in delayed payments. Do you have some sort of ongoing audit procedure in place to check the accuracy of your invoicing? The twenty seconds it takes to cross-reference invoice details with the original order is a small price to pay for accurate billing and prompt payments. Don't give your customers an excuse to slow down the payment process by sending them an inaccurate invoice—and multiplying your payment delays.

Date invoices

This may sound really simple but don't forget to indicate on your invoices the date that payment is due. I once forgot to do this and when I rang the customer to ask where the payment was, they said their invoice had no payment date on it. I looked at our copy and sure enough, there was no due-by date on the invoice.

Give sufficient information on invoices

Many companies use purchase order numbers or supplier identifier numbers when ordering a product. Ensure you put all this information on invoices in a clear and identifiable way, so that there is no hold-up in the processing of payment.

Send invoices to the right people

Make sure invoices are sent to the right person for immediate approval. To increase your chances of this occurring, include on the invoice the name of the person who made the order. In many instances, companies will send invoices directly to the purchasing or accounting department. The invoice is then transferred to the appropriate person or department for approval before being sent back to the accounting team for payment, causing even further delays.

199. Automate for prompt billing

I've mentioned the importance of having an efficient and simple billing process in place to enable invoices to be generated and mailed quickly. As your business grows and becomes more successful, you may not be able to keep up with the demand if you continue to process invoices manually. This is when modern technology comes to your aid. There are a number of invoicing software programs that you can purchase off the shelf from software suppliers. Many of these are more than adequate for most small businesses. Alternatively, you may wish to see if there is any billing software available specifically for your type of business and industry. If not, consider having some developed. While there is initial cost in doing so, an efficient billing system will more than pay for itself in terms of accelerated cash flow.

200. Offer an incentive for early payments

Are you able to offer an incentive for early payments made by your customers? Some companies offer a 10 per cent discount for up-front cash payments, or a discount for payments made within 14 days of purchase.

Susan operates an event management company that specialises in conferences for large associations and corporate organisations. Given the nature of her work, there are a large number of bills that need to be confirmed and paid for well before the event actually takes place. These include the event venue, catering and hotel accommodation. The challenge Susan and other professionals in her field constantly face is trying to confirm delegate attendance numbers as early as possible. Therefore, to encourage participants to register and make payment well in advance, most events offer an 'early bird' registration fee that could be up to 15 per cent cheaper than later registration.

While you are giving away some revenue by offering these discounts, it is a small price to pay for having cash in the bank—and it is a lot cheaper than the cost, time and stress of chasing up late payments. If you do offer early payment discounts, display them prominently on your invoice.

201. Charge for late payments

As an alternative to rewarding customers for paying early, consider the worth of charging them interest on overdue accounts. Make sure any penalties you impose are written into the relevant contracts and are well publicised to customers. These strategies often assist in creating urgency among customers to ensure the payment is made on time.

When I first entered into the lease arrangement for my computer, I was fined for an overdue payment. The computer was being paid for by direct debit; however, due to an administrative bungle the collection agency was not notified of my new bank account details. As a result, their attempts to collect the payment were rejected and I incurred a fine of $25. I had to accept the fine as it was my fault, but I was still not happy about having to fork out an extra $25. Suffice to say, the fine did the trick as far as the collection agency was concerned. Since that encounter they have happily collected all subsequent payments from me, on time and with no hassle.

202. Take a deposit to get the payment process underway

Hotels, tailors, photographers, function centres, clothing hire stores, caterers, airlines and builders are just some of the businesses that require their customers to pay an up-front deposit before they will begin any work. Deposits are a great idea as they commit the customer to the buying process and assist in covering any up-front expenses incurred by your business. In many cases, deposits can be refunded within a certain time period, after which an administration fee is deducted. The closer it gets to the specified date, the higher the administration fee becomes. In some businesses, the deposit paid by the customer is non-refundable: if the customer cancels the transaction, they lose the whole deposit amount. Can you incorporate an up-front deposit into your business?

203. Accounts payable staff are your best friends

Here's a strategy to ensure you get paid on time straight from the school of how to win friends and influence people. Be sure to develop a close but professional relationship with the accounts payable people within the businesses that owe you money. With small operators, this may be the owner themselves. If a payment hasn't been received, ask whether there is anything you can do to assist in speeding up the process. Businesses that are short on cash are constantly making decisions about whom to pay first, and by staying in close contact, you are more likely to be in this category.

Paying the bills

It's important for your business to pay all its bills on time as this maintains a good relationship with your suppliers and creates a marketable credit rating that you can leverage to your advantage in other transactions. While it may seem like a contradiction in terms, your business can save money by paying bills. Here are a few ideas to show you how.

204. Watch for errors in the invoices you receive

As highlighted in the previous section, suppliers (your own business included) can sometimes make mistakes when preparing invoices. Think of all the errors you have discovered when checking shop, hotel or restaurant bills. The same process applies in your business. Always check every bill and wherever possible, have the person who initiated the purchase carefully review and approve any invoices before payment is made. Those without knowledge of the transaction probably won't have enough information to catch errors in quantity, pricing, discounts, terms and calculations.

> *Recently I received an order from a customer with a cheque for $76. I processed the order, packaged his goods, prepared an invoice and sent everything off in the mail the very same day. One week later I received a photocopy of my original invoice from the same customer with a cheque for another $76. I cross-referenced the invoice against my records and confirmed that I had already received payment one week earlier. I decided to call my customer to clarify what had happened. I soon discovered that on receiving my package, the secretary had placed the manuals and invoice in her manager's in-tray. Without checking the invoice other than looking at the total owed, the boss had approved it and sent it off to accounts for payment. Interestingly, this invoice had been approved for payment again even though the words 'thank you for your payment' were emblazoned across the middle in bold type along with the date payment had been received and the cheque number.*

It is surprising how often an invoice error goes unnoticed, leaving you to pay more than is necessary.

205. Watch out for phantom invoices

If you do not check your invoices thoroughly, you are leaving your business wide open for abuse by unscrupulous suppliers and con artists. Unfortunately, when your business deals with a number of suppliers and contractors, there is the possibility of receiving incorrect invoices or invoices for products that were never ordered. In most cases these represent honest mistakes. In some cases, however, an unscrupulous supplier has decided to try and sneak an invoice through and collect for a product never delivered or services never rendered. There are also a number of invoicing scams where phantom invoices are sent to companies for small amounts of money; because the amount requested is small, many companies just gloss over it and pay the invoice. However, to the unscrupulous operator, $10 from 10 000 companies is a nice pay packet.

You can avoid becoming the victim of such scams in the following ways.

■ Implement a purchasing system whereby nothing is ordered without your business issuing an order number. If you receive an invoice without an order number, you don't pay it until the supplier provides the correct details.

■ All invoices are to be approved by the employee who ordered the goods or services.

■ All supporting documentation such as the original quotes from at least three suppliers, pricing list and product details should be attached to the approved invoice for cross-referencing by the individual responsible for issuing the payment.

206. Ask suppliers for early payment terms

In the previous section, I mentioned how your business could offer discounts for early payments as a way of encouraging suppliers to pay their bills on time. If you are in a position to pay your accounts early, use this strategy to your advantage and negotiate with your suppliers for an up-front payment discount when negotiating the payment terms of your supply agreement.

207. Don't make payments until you have to

If your supplier doesn't offer a worthwhile incentive to pay early, then don't pay until the due date. In my experience as both a supplier and a customer, this strategy is very common among most businesses. And it makes sense too—you might as well let the money sit in your account earning interest for you as long as possible rather than earning it for your supplier. Of course, it's important that you do pay by the due date in order to protect your credit rating and reputation. This is where Internet banking or direct debiting from your account is so useful. These methods of payment allow you to keep your money in your account right up to the day payment is due and then with the click of a few buttons the money is transferred and the bill is paid.

208. When money is tight and you still have bills to pay

There will be at least one occasion in the life of every business when there is simply not enough money coming in to meet all the expenses. Alternatively, you may have a number of large bills to pay all at the same time and to do so under your normal terms of business would severely deplete your cash reserves. The following ideas will help you stay on top of your bills without incurring further costs.

Ask for credit

If you have an excellent payment record with your suppliers, speak to them about extending credit to you. While no business likes to offer credit, no business likes to lose a good customer, so many of your suppliers may decide to support you in your time of need.

Ask for split payment terms

In effect, this is similar to taking a small loan and it's not uncommon for some suppliers to offer these extended billing terms, essentially allowing for payment to be made over a period of time such as ninety days. If you receive these terms, you will be required to pay a third of the amount within thirty days, another third in sixty days and the balance at ninety days. There is generally no interest charged for this system unless you default on one or more of the payments.

Get your credit card to work for you

Do you have a large number of bills due around the same time every month? Well, here is a trick I learned from an ex-employee who used to work in a major international bank. If you normally pay these bills by credit card, contact your bank and change your billing cycle so that it ends the day before the debits occur. In doing so, you will give yourself the full 55 days interest-free period in which to settle the accounts.

Talk to your suppliers

Communicating your situation honestly and openly with your suppliers is essential to the survival of any small business. But don't just tell them what the problems are, talk to them as a partnership about how both of you are going to overcome these challenges and ensure all the bills are paid and both businesses flourish. If one of your suppliers decides to abandon you, don't fret. Unless they are operating in a monopoly market, there will be plenty of others who will be willing to take their place.

There are many astute business operators who actually use all of these strategies on a daily basis despite the fact they have loads of money in the bank. Their goal is to hold on to their cash for as long as possible, making it do the maximum work for them before they have to give it away.

11

OFFICE AND BUSINESS PREMISES

Your place of business can be your biggest asset or your biggest liability. The choice is yours. Choosing the right location for your business provides a solid foundation from which to grow and succeed in your chosen industry. However, a good location still doesn't guarantee business success. Prime locations often come with high expenses attached and it is these ongoing costs that could be the ruin of your business. This chapter explores a number of ideas that will help you keep the cost of having a place of business under control.

Chapter 11

Office and business premises

This chapter covers:

209. Renegotiate your lease

If you find your lease is due for renewal and the real estate market is on the soft side then make the most of this opportunity to renegotiate your lease.

Jaswant and Kartar Singh are the regional operators for Kirby vacuum cleaners in Malaysia. During the economic crisis that hit Asia in the mid to late 90s the Singh brothers found the lease on their office was due to expire. Businesses were closing down by the hundreds each week and most office buildings were experiencing extremely high levels of vacancies. Many of those who were still in business were finding it tough to pay their rent. The boys took the opportunity to renegotiate their lease with the owner and came up with a great deal. Total savings on their office rental were around $3000 a year.

210. Request more free rent

A standard part of almost any lease negotiation is a period of free rental within the first year of your agreement. If you are about to renew an existing lease or sign up for a brand new one, consider asking for more than the standard four weeks rent-free. For example, Geoff recently signed a three-year lease for his business located in the centre of the city that provided him with two months free rental in the first year and a further one month in each consecutive year. If the landlord is unable or unwilling to give a complete month for free, ask for two or three weeks free rental.

Johnson leases an outlet in a large suburban shopping centre. When negotiating his lease he managed to secure a rent-free period of six weeks—two weeks more than the standard one month usually offered. Johnson described the outcome saying, 'I'll take whatever I can negotiate. While I didn't get the eight weeks I wanted, I'd rather have the extra two weeks for free than have to pay for them. Free is free regardless of how big or little the amount'.

In many instances, this is often the easiest negotiating point for landlords to offer you as an incentive so make sure you try to capitalise on it as much as possible. Remember, free is free!

211. Size does matter when calculating your rentable space

Many leases are calculated based on a set amount per square metre. It is therefore extremely important to your bottom line to verify the accuracy of the square meterage specified as the rentable space on which your rent is calculated. Measure your space carefully and compare it with the total area specified in your lease. Many office spaces and shop lots are unusually shaped so keep an eye out for all those nooks and crannies that are often considered part of the floor space but are really difficult to use.

Gary runs a chain of well-known jewellery stores. While negotiating the lease for a new 'express counter' at a suburban shopping centre, Gary discovered the centre management were charging him for the complete surface area of the outlet. The unusual location of the outlet meant it had a number of sharp pointed corners that could not be used for anything. There was also an external staircase at one end that protruded into the rented area. The open space underneath the staircase could not be used for anything other than storage. Gary put forward his argument to the centre management that these particular areas were considered dead space and for them to become functional areas, he would have to spend a considerable amount of his own money. After some negotiation, the management agreed to remove the area caused by the sharp corners from the rentable floor space, reducing the leased area by two square metres. This small reduction in space resulted in a saving of over $1200 a year in rent for Gary and his new outlet.

212. What is everyone else paying?

Before you sign the lease, do some research on the terms and conditions that other tenants are receiving and the concessions they have been able to negotiate. Often this is not as difficult as it sounds. In my experience, tenants are willing to share information among each other in the hope of finding out something that will assist them in getting a better deal. Also, try to uncover any plans a tenant may have for moving. Armed with this information, you can use the lowest net rentals and lease terms as the basis for your negotiations. When comparing rents, keep in mind they can vary considerably within the same building, depending on the size of the office, the floor level, whether there are any views, and if there is street frontage or you are overlooking the car park.

213. Get an expert's advice

This is one area where I encourage you to spend a bit of money up-front to save you a lot of money in the long run. Get a lawyer or lease consultant with extensive experience in the commercial real estate market to review your lease agreement and clarify any onerous and possibly costly contract terms. It would also be a wise move to have your accountant and insurer review the relevant portions of the lease agreement and put forward workable solutions for reducing your overheads. If you are planning on doing any renovations or fit-outs to the space, it may be worthwhile having your contractor take a look at the specific sections of the agreement.

214. Ensure you get what you paid for

If you are situated in a shopping centre or office building, the lease may contain additional charges for the management of common areas. Firstly, ensure the lease clearly indicates a maximum cap on your share of these operating costs. This will prevent the landlord from raising them to unreasonable levels during the course of the year. Secondly, make sure the landlord is using this money for the intended purposes. If common areas such as lift lobbies, hallways and toilet facilities are not cleaned and maintained to an acceptable standard, start making some noise. Make your landlord accountable and have them show you where your fees are being spent. Retailers situated in a shopping complex may also be charged for general advertising and promotion expenses. These funds should be used by centre management to attract more customers through the promotion of the complex as a special shopping destination.

Paul, Michelle and Ethan all owned and operated retail outlets in a medium-sized suburban shopping complex. As part of their lease agreement, they were required to pay a levy for general advertising and promotion costs. Business had been fairly slow over the past couple of months and all three had noticed a distinct fall in the number of shoppers walking through the shopping centre. Other tenants had also noticed that the regular advertising feature that used to appear in the local newspaper had been absent in the last four editions and there didn't seem to be as many events or activities happening within the complex to attract shoppers. The three tenants approached the shopping centre management, requesting details of how their advertising and promotion money was being spent. A promotion schedule was given to the tenants; however, most of the strategies indicated in it had not occurred. Despite protests from the centre management that the money was being spent in the correct manner, the tenants hired a lawyer to follow up the matter, who soon discovered the centre management had been withholding tenants' advertising and promotion funds for their own profit. The centre management refunded the advertising and promotion fee to all tenants for the relevant period. In addition, a working group of centre management and tenant representatives was established to develop and manage all future expenditure of the advertising and promotion levy.

If your building is located in an older building, steer clear of lease agreements that permit any renovation costs to be charged as operating expenses to be shared among all tenants. You could find yourself being party to a rather large bill for any structural works being undertaken.

215. Persistence pays in getting a reduction

In business as in life, there is one quality that is the cornerstone to all success—persistence. To get a rent reduction, enter into a planned and persistent campaign directed at your landlord. Write to them periodically and ask for a rent reduction based on factual economic justification.

Brenda operated her small travel agency from a large suburban shopping centre. In recent months, she had experienced a huge decline in business due to the terrorist attacks of September 11, the collapse of a major airline and the unwillingness of people to travel anywhere. She had made numerous requests to the centre management for a reduction in her rent, with reviews to be held after three and six months. After the management's initial refusal, Brenda set about a campaign to justify her request on pure economic grounds. She cut out every relevant article she could find from newspapers and magazines on how recent events had affected the travel industry and sent these to the centre manager with a covering note. She scanned the Internet and forwarded any relevant items to him by email. A number of other travel agents in the area had recently closed down, so she made sure he was aware of this and provided him with all the specific details. Brenda even invited the centre manager to attend a special meeting being held by travel industry representatives to develop strategies for keeping their businesses afloat. And to top it all off, she provided him with certified financial statements of income and expenditure for her business comparing the three months leading up to the events and the three months after. Brenda's persistence and ingenuity finally won her the rent reprieve she required to keep her business in business.

216. Become a landlord

Are your business premises too big for your needs? If they are then take a proactive approach to reduce your rental expenses by renting out your extra space. And don't limit yourself to office space. The following examples demonstrate how some businesses have found ways to put any extra space to good use.

Ron owns a family law firm in the centre of the city and leases out two adjacent offices under the one lease. By doing so he has increased the area he is leasing and is able to command a lower rental. Within the lease agreement he included the option to sublet one of the offices, which he subsequently did. The rental he receives for the second office is higher than what he is paying for it but still very attractive to prospective tenants. And I should know because I was one of them.

Trevor's business owned the three-storey inner city office complex that also housed his own office. The building included a serviced kitchen area and fully equipped meeting facilities with a boardroom which could comfortably fit twenty people around a large mahogany table and was primarily used to hold the company's quarterly board meetings. Realising this was a wasted resource, Trevor set about marketing the boardroom facilities to nearby businesses. The response was excellent and he regularly has about three companies by a week paying to hire out his boardroom.

Lisa operates her own very successful physiotherapy business located in a renovated house. The house proved ideal premises as each room was converted into separate treatment areas along with a spacious reception. However, the five converted rooms proved too many for her practice, so she placed an advert in a health publication, offering a room to rent. Lisa was inundated with responses and finally settled on a podiatrist who had just started his own business. The decision proved a good one as both businesses benefited from the referral of clients to each other. It also helped Lisa significantly reduce her monthly rent.

Philip's accounting firm kicked off twelve months before the introduction of the GST and BAS requirements for business so he was guaranteed to have plenty of work to keep him busy. He rented an office close to a semi-industrial area where a large proportion of his clients would be located. The office was larger than he required; however, the price was a bargain so he took it. At the same time, a friend from his university days was setting up her own financial planning business and was looking for a place to locate. The synergy of an accounting firm and a financial planner was a good one and Philip's friend quickly agreed to rent a desk within the office.

As part of her office lease, Andrea receives a secure car parking space within the building. Living only one train stop from the office, Andrea chooses to either take public transport or walk to work, instead of using her car. Given the high demand for secure parking within the city, Andrea decided to rent her parking space to another *tenant within the building. The money she receives for a month's car parking is the equivalent of one week's rental on her office, saving her $5500 a year.*

217. Serviced offices

The concept of the serviced office has been around for over a decade; however, only in the last five years has this format become a popular alternative for many businesses. More efficient workspace design, building design and associated services have resulted in flexible office premises that cater for the different phases of a business's growth. When seeking commercial office space, many businesses often fail to consider all the costs associated with it, including fit-out, furniture, infrastructure for technology and communication services, and building outgoings. These added expenses can easily double the actual cost of the space you are looking to rent.

One of the main selling points of serviced offices is they cater for the cycle of growth and contraction in size that many businesses experience. If a company needs to expand, they can simply take up more office space within the same building. This saves the company having to pay for relocation and fit-out costs that would be required when moving to a new location. As they maintain the same address and contact details, there is also no need to reprint new business stationery such as letterhead, envelopes and business cards, and time and money are saved by not having to inform customers and suppliers of their new address. The tenants have the option of signing short-term leases with six months being the minimum term accepted, so they do not have to worry about overcommitting to a long lease arrangement. The tenants range from sole operators to small businesses with up to thirty employees. Businesses located in a serviced office enjoy the added advantage of a prestigious location and image without the expensive price tag.

The following is an example of how a business can create major problems for itself by undertaking normal lease arrangements.

In its early years of operation, a small computer firm with twelve staff leased an office in a serviced office building. With the boom in the IT industry, this particular company experienced tremendous growth and grew to over 120 employees within twelve months. The management decided to rent out two complete floors in a neighbouring *building and signed a six-year lease agreement. The fit-out costs alone were around $8 million. When the bottom fell out of the IT world, the company suffered enormous losses. Of the original 120 staff, only fifteen remained. There was still three years remaining on the watertight lease and the company had to write off about $10 million in outstanding rent and fit-out costs.*

218. Pay your rent as a percentage of your sales

Here's a bright idea that could save you literally thousands of dollars on the rental of your business premises. Instead of paying a set monthly figure, negotiate with the landlord to pay them a percentage of your revenue. The percentage to be paid is calculated on gross revenue earned, usually over a three-month period in the first instance and then monthly after that. Therefore, the more successful your business is, the more rent the landlord will receive. You need to put forward a very strong case to prove you will be able to achieve the projected revenue targets that you presented to the landlord. The benefit for the tenant is twofold. Firstly, you don't have the initial rental expenses that you would have to pay under a normal lease agreement. You can then use this money in a proactive manner to generate more business. Secondly, if times are tough then your chances of survival are given a big boost, as your rental overheads will be minimal.

Wayne operated a successful antique furniture business from home for a number of years. In an endeavour to stimulate further sales and increase his visibility, he decided to open a retail outlet in a quiet shopping arcade attached to a five-star hotel. His products were particularly appealing to the Japanese and Korean market, which constituted many of the hotel's guests. Moving into unknown territory, he found himself having to deal with the additional costs of fitting out his shop lot, paying for sales staff and transporting the furniture to the new outlet. Concerned that his initial costs were too high, Wayne spoke with the landlord and negotiated a different type of lease arrangement. While he still paid an up-front deposit, Wayne would not be charged a set rental fee each month. Instead, he would pay a percentage of his total revenue before expenses every three months. The landlord was happy as he was able to lease out an outlet that had been vacant for some time, while Wayne significantly reduced his overheads by negotiating a rental based on actual sales.

219. Let your business be lured to a location

Many communities offer a wide range of incentives to lure businesses into their area. If you are not constrained by specific geographic location, it could be worth your while financially to set up operations within a specific development zone. In many cases, businesses can benefit from tax incentives, low interest loans, reductions in utility costs and lower land rates. Some communities even offer ancillary benefits such as free memberships to golf clubs and fitness centres.

When Sandra was searching for new headquarters for her recruitment company, she deliberately chose not to rent. Instead, she took full advantage of low property values in a fast-developing regional community and secured a 25 per cent reduction in building rates. She also made the most of a $75 000 loan contributed by the local economic development authority to upgrade her new premises, while paying a very low rate of interest.

Andrew was also lured to set up operations in a regional area. His manufacturing company would generate over fifty full-time jobs for the local community and would hopefully be the catalyst for more medium-sized industries to establish themselves in the area. As an incentive, he was offered free land rates for the first three years of operation along with free rental of a council-owned house for his family for the same period.

220. Your business location can reduce your overall expenses

It's true. The first three rules to business success are location, location and location. Your location can be the launching pad from which you build your success. By establishing your business in a particular area, you can save on other expenses.

Claire owns a cafe located in the centre of the city. High-rise office buildings full of hungry employees surround her very popular outlet. Great food and friendly service bring people thronging to her business every day. In the three years she has owned the cafe, Claire has not spent a single cent on advertising and promotion, yet her sales and profit have increased by 35 per cent.

Tony moved his call centre from the suburbs to a city location, costing him an extra $200 a month in rent. So why did he move if it is more expensive? Well, the money he saves on recruitment costs quickly offsets the money Tony spends on extra rent. Previously, Tony found it difficult to get people to travel out to his suburban office because of the distance and inconvenience—it required a number of different trains and/or buses to get there. As many of his staff were university students or travellers, this presented unnecessary hassle and extra public transport costs. He was spending over $400 a month placing recruitment ads, not to mention the time and energy every week recruiting and training new employees. By locating in the city, he found it was necessary to recruit only once every five to six weeks.

221. Your ego and office space savings

Just how big and spacious an office do you need? If your customers rarely, if ever, come to your office, it makes little sense to spend money on elaborate and spacious offices until your business is highly successful. Even then, I would question the sense of business people who seem content to waste money on building small empires for themselves. Do you need an office with views of the beach or harbour? Do you need to be located on the higher floors? Is locating in the centre of the city really going to improve your bottom line or can you make do with an office in the suburbs?

The lease on the expansive offices occupied by Carmen's public relations firm was coming to an end and the landlord was keen to have her re-sign for a further term. Carmen noticed a similar-sized *office space had become available on the same floor with the only difference being the office had no windows. When she inquired with the landlord, she discovered the new office would be $5000 a year less than what she was currently paying. People obviously didn't like the idea of not being able to see daylight. This was not a problem for Carmen and her team, who then spent a weekend repainting the office in bright colours that gave it a real air of fun and excitement. They also installed a fish tank and bought some lively prints to hang on the walls. The final touch was some indoor plants, and the lack of windows no longer seemed an issue. By spending just under $1000 to redecorate the office, Carmen saved her company $4000 a year in rent.*

222. The home office

Many of you reading this book are probably just like the millions of other small business owners around the world who operate a home business. Contrary to popular belief, operating a business from home is not just for those starting out as their own boss. Many business owners have been successfully running operations from their home office for many years. My accountant, Sue, has been operating her accountancy firm from home for over ten years. Andy has turned a $100 investment into a $200 000 mail order business managed entirely from his inner city apartment. Sheree enjoys the benefits of mixing business and leisure by running her public relations business from her home study for the past seven years.

Whether you are working from your garage, your spare bedroom or the kitchen table, the home office offers your business many cost-saving advantages. Consider the following savings you will make by basing your business from home.

Tax deductions

These are numerous and varied so it's best to consult your accountant, but it will be worth it.

Rent

By locating at home you are saving on the office rental you would normally have to pay.

Furniture

Many home offices consist of cardboard boxes for storage cabinets, bricks and wooden planks for bookshelves and a trestle table for a desk. Functionality is the aim for most home businesses, saving a good deal on office furniture.

Transport

The furthest you may have to travel each day will be from the bedroom to kitchen table. No more traffic jams, train or bus fares, parking fees or petrol costs.

Time

Less travelling means more time to spend on making your business a success.

223. Don't have an office at all

The advent of computers, the Internet, mobile phones and other pieces of technology has significantly reduced the need for office premises, to the point where many business people don't even have an office. As mentioned in the previous point, there are many entrepreneurs who run highly successful businesses from home. But what do they do when they have to meet an important client, their bank manager or a potential investor? Surely they don't invite them home and sit around the kitchen table to discuss that $200 000 loan? Well, some small business operators I know do exactly that. However, if you are not comfortable with this homely approach to conducting business, try the following, each illustrated below.

Meet the client at their business

Angela is a very talented seamstress who has turned her skills into a highly successful curtain business. She specialises in crafting elegant drapes and curtains of any size and design for corporate offices, hotels, serviced apartments and private dwellings. Angela's office is a double roller door garage at the back of her suburban home—not the ideal showroom to host her well-to-do clientele. To overcome the need for a fancy and expensive showroom, Angela always meets her clients at their premises and she has adapted her display items and material swatches so they can all fit into a medium-sized trolley that can be easily pushed around from job to job and sits nicely in the back of her four-wheel drive.

Become a virtual tenant

Fiona runs her own small recruitment company. Image is an important part of this industry and many companies spend a large proportion of their budget on plush offices and meeting facilities located in the heart of the city's business district. To overcome this dilemma, Fiona has signed on as a virtual tenant with a business centre. When customers telephone her, the business centre receptionist, who introduces herself using Fiona's company name, answers the call. All calls are then diverted to Fiona's mobile or house phone and the customer is none the wiser. Fiona maintains the image of a large and successful recruitment company for the measly sum of $1000 a month.

Meet at a neutral venue

Natalie is a well-regarded executive coach working with middle and senior managers to be the very best they can be at whatever profession they are in. She operates her business from home and is reticent to have her clients meet her there, because she feels it does not complement the image her business successfully portrays. Alternatively, meeting at the clients' place of work is fraught with distractions. As a workable compromise, Natalie and her clients meet in the lobby or coffee lounge of five-star hotels located within the city. The plush and quiet surrounds make for the ideal place to conduct business.

Rent a meeting room

James has struck a deal with an office building to hire out their meeting room on an ad hoc basis. He conducts strategic planning workshops with his client companies and prefers to use a venue that is both private and away from the clients' normal place of business. His actual office is the study of his three-bedroom apartment and probably not the most appropriate place to conduct sessions with his customers. James believes the small cost of hiring the meeting rooms far outweighs the expenses involved in a hefty lease agreement.

12

BANKING, TAXATION AND INSURANCE

Banks, tax and insurance are the bane of many business operators—but every cloud has a silver lining. While these factors are a reality of doing business in today's marketplace, there are a number of strategies you can implement to minimise their cost impact on your business. This chapter will give you an insight into how to get the biggest savings from managing your money.

TAX FORM

Chapter 12

Banking, taxation and insurance

This chapter covers:

Your bank and your business

224. Shop around for the best bank rates and service

225. How's your banking relationship?

226. Be honest with your banker

227. Develop an excellent credit rating

228. Bank service charges

229. Have enough money in the bank

230. Bank money straight away

231. Fast deposit your way to savings

232. Renegotiate your credit card merchant fees

Your accountant

233. Get a good accountant

234. Don't trust your local bar stool accountant

235. Accountants read balance sheets, not minds

236. Keeping your accountant affordable

237. Do a basic bookkeeping course

Tax savings

238. Keep track of all receipts

239. GST savings

240. FBT savings

241. Buy more and sell less to save on tax

242. Pay your taxes on time

Insurance

243. Shop around annually

244. Make changes to your business to cut insurance costs

245. Reduce risks to reduce costs

Your bank and your business

Like it or not, very few small to medium businesses can survive without the assistance of the banks. Whatever your feelings are towards them and the financial community in general, banks provide a vital service to virtually every business in the country. The first step towards getting the most out of your bank is to make sure you choose the right one. These ideas help you do so, and show that by working within the systems and structures set up by banks, you can maximise your interest and lending potential and minimise the costly fees your business can incur.

224. Shop around for the best bank rates and service

Banking is a very competitive business and like any business, the rates, charges and levels of service can differ significantly from bank to bank. Look at your relationship with your bank and ask yourself if you are happy with the level of service you are receiving. Are you paying too much in fees and charges for your business accounts? If you are then don't be afraid to shop around for a lower rate. Look for a bank that offers competitive fees and provides a high level of service to their customers. How interested do you think your bank manager is in your business? There's only one sure way to find out and that is to ask them to reduce the fees and charges you pay on your account. Never let a bank make you feel like they are doing you a favour by allowing you to put your money with them.

225. How's your banking relationship?

A good banking relationship is a partnership of sorts. Some lending officers understand that there can be difficult times and they work with their clients to help them through these times. Other banks have an ultra-conservative culture and become very nervous when a client experiences some financial difficulty. As a business you shouldn't have to worry that at the first sign of financial stress the bank will put unreasonable pressure on you or will bail out completely. Look for a bank that has a strong history of working through tough situations with its clients. Talk to other business contacts and ask them what banks they use and why they use them.

226. Be honest with your banker

The relationship your business has with its lending partner is a vital element in managing your company. While you might not need to borrow money now, you could well do in the future. A common mistake that some businesses make is not being totally honest with their bank.

John secured a loan of $150 000 to achieve a life-long dream of owning a restaurant. Unfortunately, the restaurant trade wasn't as exciting and glamorous as he had first imagined and the realities of running such a business really hit home. After the first three months business was less than encouraging, and having to meet the ongoing costs of wages, rent, supplies, power and water, left barely enough to pay for any promotion or advertising, let alone meet loan repayments. John contacted his bank immediately and arranged a meeting with the loans manager. After a lengthy discussion the loans manager agreed to restructure John's loan, reducing the monthly repayments. Of course, this was based on John fulfilling a number of conditions, including drawing up a plan as to how he was going to resurrect his business.

Your bank needs to know when there are problems. Springing a surprise on the bank puts a big dent in your credibility and the relationship suffers.

227. Develop an excellent credit rating

What sort of credit rating does your business have? Do you pay your suppliers on time? Are your credit card bills paid in full or do you only make the minimum payment required? How well do you service any loans you may have? Are you regularly meeting repayments or constantly being hassled by the bank for that last overdue instalment? If you have a bad credit rating, it will be difficult for you to borrow money when you most need it.

When Brett was 16 and still at school, his uncle advised him to take out a $2000 loan from the bank as soon as he got his first full-time job. As a hard-up teenager, Brett got very excited at the thought of this amount of money, but his visions of spending it all on a car, holiday or good times were soon shattered by his uncle's next suggestion: to put the borrowed money aside in a separate savings account and then pay off the loan over a six-month period. Once *that loan was paid, the next step would be to borrow $5000 and repeat the process. By participating in this activity, Brett would create a positive credit history that he could later use to secure a much larger loan for a house or finance a business. Brett followed his uncle's advice, and by the time he was twenty-five he had borrowed and successfully paid off over $70 000 in loans. Five years later Brett decided to open his own plumbing business; he went to the bank and easily secured a $50 000 loan to purchase a van and all the necessary equipment. His excellent credit history gave Brett the advantage he needed to live out his dream of being his own boss.*

228. Bank service charges

Despite what most people think, it doesn't cost very much to keep your money in a bank account. It's when you start to use the money in your account that the fees and charges apply. Unfortunately, there is no escaping bank fees and charges at the present time as all the banks have them, so consider these ideas to keep the expenses of running your bank account to a minimum.

Study the terms and conditions

Before signing on to a particular bank or account type, be sure to review all bank documentation regarding service fees and charges. Then choose the account that will best suit your needs.

Use your own bank only

Use your own bank for ATM withdrawals and account inquiries, as you will be charged a fee for these at a competitor's bank.

Take out enough to cover a number of expenses

All accounts charge a fee if you make more than the allocated number of withdrawals each month. To reduce these transactions costs, use the Internet or combine multiple payments to one supplier. If you purchase goods for $50 and $235 from the same supplier within the space of a few weeks, combine the bills and pay the full $285 in one go.

Don't use the bank teller

Gone are the days of having a chat to the friendly bank teller. I imagine they are still friendly, though I wouldn't really know as I haven't used one in such a long time—they're just too damn expensive. Most banks now charge a ridiculous fee every time you have a bank teller assist you with a transaction.

Bank over the Net

If you are not doing it by now, you should be. Get yourself and your bank accounts hooked up to do Internet banking. This enables you to transfer funds between your own accounts, plus to other people's accounts. Some banks do not charge any fees for Internet banking, regardless of the number of transactions you perform.

Use cash for small amounts

Many cheque accounts charge you for issuing an excessive amount of cheques within a month. I know a number of businesses that won't write a cheque for anything less than $100: they'd rather pay cash or do a direct debit straight into the customer's account.

Avoid statement charges

Are you being charged for having bank statements posted out to you? If so advise your bank to stop sending out statements. It's easier and cheaper to log onto your account over the Internet and print off a statement as and when required.

Keep a minimum monthly balance

If your account requires you to have a minimum monthly balance, ensure you know what that balance is and keep enough money in there to avoid hefty charges.

Don't have too many accounts

How many bank accounts does your business actually need? Each individual account increases the account and transaction fees and government charges—not to mention the time and money spent balancing the books.

Be aware that banks sometimes make mistake

Regularly check your account and credit card statements and don't just accept the fees and charges if they appear to be too high. If it doesn't look right, contact the bank and ask them to explain.

Like it or not, bank fees and charges are a necessary evil of doing business. And while the amounts individually seem small, they can soon add up to a few hundred dollars over the course of a year. However, with a bit of planning and management you can keep your costs down to the bare minimum.

229. Have enough money in the bank

Carefully monitor your cash flow and bank balances to ensure there is enough money in your account to meet all your expenses. The last thing you want to do is throw away that hard-earned money on charges for overdrawing your account. While many banks will allow your account to go into a negative balance, you end up being charged a hefty fine for the privilege.

When Peter set up his résumé writing business, he organised for all his regular bills to be deducted directly from his business account. These included the lease for his computer, Internet rental and mobile phone bill. What Peter didn't count on was the lack of revenue he would generate in the first few months to cover these bills. As a result, his account was overdrawn two months in succession and each time he incurred a fee of $35 charged by the bank. The first quarter of his business had not even passed and he had already paid more bank fees than he probably should have for the whole year.

230. Bank money straight away

Do you bank cash and cheques daily? Don't do what a friend of mine does and leave each day's takings lying around the office until he *feels like* going down to the bank. Aside from the chance of losing it (imagine the embarrassment of having to go back to a customer and ask for another cheque because you lost the first one), your money should be in the bank earning interest. When I started my self-publishing mail order business, I was over the moon every time I received cheques in the mail or credit card orders over the phone or fax. Money, money, money—I loved it, and I made sure it was banked straight away. Regular deposits not only create motivation through seeing your bottom line grow, they also demonstrate you have a consistent and healthy cash flow and make it easier to balance your books at the end of each financial period, saving you or your accountant time and money.

231. Fast deposit your way to savings

It was a really hot summer's day and I had a cash box full of cheques. It was time to do some banking so I braved the afternoon sun and made the five-minute walk to the local branch of my bank. Inside was a line of people snaking all the way from the counters to the front door. As I stood in line, I thought of all the productive things I could have been doing instead. Finally after twenty minutes it was my turn, and I stepped hot and bothered up to the counter, handing over my wad of cheques and the deposit slip to the teller. With a grin that could launch a thousand ships, she declared, 'Sir, if you are only depositing cheques then simply put them in our fast deposit envelopes and drop them in the box at the front of the branch—that way you don't have to stand in line.' I learned my lesson!

Many businesses, particularly those in mail order, receive a lot of cheques and money orders as payment for their goods and services. The fast deposit system mentioned above means you simply place cheques, money orders and a deposit slip into the special envelope provided, seal it and then drop the envelope into the fast deposit box normally located just inside the entrance of the bank. No more queues and no more wasted time.

232. Renegotiate your credit card merchant fees

If your business accepts credit card payments, you should do everything you can to drive as much business through this payment method as possible. Place stickers on your windows, door and cash register displaying the types of cards you accept. Get your staff to ask customers if they'd like to pay by credit card. Place the credit card machine in a prominent place on your counter. The more business you do using credit cards, the more cost-effective it becomes for your business. Firstly, every business is charged a monthly bank fee for the use of their credit card facility. The more transactions you make, the lower the cost per sale this fee becomes. For example, if your monthly fee was $20 and you only did twenty credit card transactions, the cost per sale of that fee is $1. However, if you did one hundred credit card sales then the cost per sale would be only 20c. Secondly, by increasing the amount of business you do through credit card transactions, your bargaining power to have merchant fees reduced becomes stronger. A simple reduction of 1 per cent could save a business thousands of dollars a year.

If you are uncertain about accepting credit cards, start off by only accepting Mastercard, Visa and Bankcard. Not only are the merchant fees associated with these cards far cheaper than American Express and Diners Club cards, they are more commonly used by everyday people. Plus, you will only be paying one monthly fee. Ensure that you clearly state on all your order forms, invoices and promotional material what credit cards you accept. There is nothing worse than receiving a large order from a new customer only to find they have given you an American Express card number that you cannot accept.

Your accountant

There is no substitute for a good accountant.

233. Get a good accountant

One of the greatest allies a business owner can have is a good accountant, so make sure you find one who will take a proactive approach to your business. When sourcing an accountant, ask to look at a list of their clients and if you notice a string of small to medium-sized businesses on their books, then there is a good chance you have found the right one. In some cases you may even be able to find an accountant who has specific experience in your particular industry or line of work.

> When he was first looking for an accountant for his small business, Mark was determined to find someone who was running their own small business. As he put it, 'What better advice can you get than from someone who's running their own business and having to deal with the same laws, policies, procedures and conditions as you are? Not only that, they're probably claiming similar deductions to me.'

Accountants can help you establish the best bookkeeping system for your business, provide advice on business strategies and best practices, and interpret complex taxation and insurance laws. Your accountant should be one of your most valuable partners in business, so use them wisely and often.

234. Don't trust your local bar stool accountant

Never take the advice of the self-proclaimed tax expert who, after a few beers, starts to offer all sorts of 'good' advice on how to beat the taxman at his own game.

I was chatting with a client one day and he mentioned that he wanted to find a new accountant because he didn't think the guy he was currently using was getting him all the deductions he was entitled to. He explained that a friend had told him he could get a 100 per cent tax rebate on the cost of entertaining his clients. Plus, any money spent on alcohol could be claimed as well. His friend said he had been doing it for years and the taxman had never queried his accounts. While I wasn't prepared to contradict my client's friend, I suggested that the best way to resolve the matter was to actually speak with his accountant.

Hearsay on how others are saving more money through their accountant makes you ask yourself, 'If they can do it, then so can I', and you conclude that your accountant is either not streetwise enough or is just plain unhelpful. If you have chosen wisely, your accountant will already be ensuring you receive all possible tax deductions; to put your mind at rest just check with them, but don't believe everything you hear.

235. Accountants read balance sheets, not minds

'My accountant never told me that!'

Have these words ever passed your lips? If so you may have forgotten a basic truth of the accountant/client relationship—your accountant can't read your mind! It's your accountant's responsibility to provide the best advice on maximising your income and on taxation reforms and tax-effective business structures that suit your specific situation. In order to do this, they have an expectation that you will supply them with all the relevant information to do the very best possible job.

Make it your responsibility to ask your accountant as many questions as you feel necessary. Regardless of how simple or far-fetched it may seem, that question could uncover a pile of savings or deductions for your business. You and your accountant are a team—to be successful you must work together to help each other achieve the same goal.

236. Keeping your accountant affordable

Many accountants base their fees on the time it takes to do the work you require. Therefore, the more services you request, the higher fees you pay. So what can you do to keep accounting costs under control? Here are some ideas my accountant gave me.

Ask how to minimise accounting costs

Talk with your accountant on how to keep your accounting costs to a minimum. They do not want to lose your business, no matter how little it may be, and they may be quite creative in finding ways to reduce your fees.

Computerise your bookkeeping

If you are using a manual bookkeeping system, switch to a computerised one. Your accountant can provide some good advice on the type of software that would be practical for your business. It will most likely be compatible with the software they are using, saving you further time and money.

Don't use your accountant for bookkeeping

Pay your accountant for accounting and tax help. Don't pay them for bookkeeping services—they're far too expensive. Instead, use an existing member of staff, employ a part-time bookkeeper or just do it yourself.

Be organised

Keep your accounting records organised. Your accountant can give you a checklist of the records that need to be sent to their office on a regular basis. By doing this you won't be wasting time searching for missing information. I set aside ten minutes (that's all it takes if you are organised) every day to update my income and expenditure ledgers and file my receipts.

Outsource the payroll

To save time and money, consider using an outside payroll service. As previously mentioned, staff wages and all the calculations required can get rather complicated and time consuming, so save yourself the hassle and leave them to the experts.

Consult your accountant first

Give your accountant a call before making any major financial investments or contractual commitments, such as entering into lease agreements, taking out insurance cover, exercising any stock options you may have or purchasing major plant or equipment items. A quick telephone call is all it may require and they shouldn't charge you for this, but if more in-depth attention is required, remember the cost of their professional advice could save you money by preventing you from making the wrong decision.

Have accounts done less frequently

How often does your accountant do your books? If they currently balance your accounts every month, see if it is feasible to reduce that to every three months, thereby reducing the fees you will need to pay.

237. Do a basic bookkeeping course

Save money by doing the majority of the books yourself for your business. Attend one of the many excellent small business bookkeeping courses, or borrow some books from the library and ask your accountant to fill in the gaps. But remember, there is no substitute for a good accountant.

Tax savings

Payroll tax, income tax, customs and excise tax, sales tax, fringe benefits tax, land tax, stamp duties, goods and services tax, licence fees, capital gains tax and even rates levied by local councils—tax is a minefield for accountants, let alone business operators. Here are some ideas to promote tax savings in your business.

238. Keep track of all receipts

Do you know what receipts you should keep as legitimate business expenses and what items you can claim for tax purposes? If you are in doubt then my suggestion is to keep *everything*—receipts, bank statements, cheque butts, deposit books. Be sure to write the reason for the purchase on the back of every receipt, then just throw them into an old shoebox for safekeeping. When tax time arrives, simply pull out all your receipts and go through them one at a time with your accountant to determine which ones you can claim.

When it comes to claiming deductions, every little bit counts. I can't remember how many times I've heard people say, 'It was only $1.50 so I didn't bother to keep the receipt'. But $1.50 a business day will give you nearly $400 worth of deductions at the end of the year, so keep receipts for everything.

239. GST savings

If your small business earns more than $50 000 per year, you must register for goods and services tax. Many accountants will advise small business operators to stay away from it as long as possible; in fact, when I first started out my accountant gave me this exact piece of advice and with good reason. By not registering for GST your business is exempt from the various reporting requirements set out by the taxation department—this factor alone has required many small businesses to spend added funds on improving their accounting software and reporting capabilities to ensure they comply with the tax office. Until such time as you are required to report you can use your time effectively to increase your revenue and reduce your expenses. The irony is, the better you are at doing these things, the quicker you will find yourself having to register for GST. Once you have registered for GST, make sure you keep accurate records and claim everything you can.

> *Tony made the mistake of submitting all petty cash expenses as gross amounts rather than net. The error wasn't noticed until eight months into the business year. As a result, Tony's business was short-changed on the GST it could claim. This mistake could have been picked up by Tony's accountant when they sat down to do his quarterly accounts.*

When any new policies are brought in by the taxation department, it would be wise to sit down with your accountant and go through the changes in detail. Find out how they will affect your business and what, if any, changes you will need to make. And if you don't understand, ask your accountant to explain it again or get yourself another accountant.

240. FBT savings

There are many expenses incurred by small businesses that would attract fringe benefits tax. If you are presently paying FBT on any items, look at alternative arrangements to save your business money.

> *Bob was paying a generous accommodation allowance to a number of his senior managers as part of their remuneration package.*

Unfortunately, Bob also had to pay almost 100 per cent fringe benefits tax on this allowance. Therefore, instead of paying $200 to each manager per week for the allowance, Bob was paying $200 plus $200 to the tax department. When new managers were employed, Bob decided to provide an alternative to the rental allowance. He increased their salary by $8000 a year and left the new employees to work out their own accommodation. This change saved Bob's company over $2000 a year in rental allowance and over $10 000 in tax.

241. Buy more and sell less to save on tax

Reduce your business's tax liability by reducing your taxable income prior to the end of the financial year. One way of doing this is to accelerate your expenses by moving forward the purchase of equipment and supplies and the payment of staff bonuses and charitable donations to just before the end of each tax period. This is one particular circumstance where spending more will actually save you money. Conversely, withhold sending invoices to your customers until after the end of the tax year to reduce your taxable income.

242. Pay your taxes on time

If you owe money to the tax department, then pay them on time to avoid being penalised. It's as simple as that.

Insurance

Insurance is an essential cost of running your small business. Unfortunately, you cannot be in business without insurance. Workers compensation, public liability, products liability, motor vehicle, burglary, income protection and life insurance are just some of the policies your business may need to have. In some cases, how much insurance you need is not entirely up to you; nevertheless there are some strategies to keep your insurance costs to a minimum.

243. Shop around annually

Don't just automatically renew your insurance without checking out what the competition is offering. Insurance companies are always offering new products and services that may surpass what you currently have. It is worthwhile employing the services of an independent insurance broker to research the best policies for your needs.

244. Make changes to your business to cut insurance costs

Insurance is a necessity but paying high premiums doesn't have to be. Insurance costs need to be managed in order to keep your premiums to a minimum. You can keep workers compensation insurance under control by implementing safety programs and systems, as mentioned in Chapter 2. Fewer claims mean lower premiums. You could also modify your facilities and services to keep premiums in check.

> *Winnie owns and manages a day care centre. The facility used to have some of the best play equipment in the neighbourhood; however, what was good for the children proved to be bad for insurance. When assessed by the insurer, she was able to save over $2000 a year on premiums by removing some of the more dangerous equipment.*

Ask your insurer to assess your business for ways to cut insurance costs. If they are not prepared to do this, then take your business elsewhere.

245. Reduce risks to reduce costs

It is almost impossible to prevent any form of injury, loss, breakage or theft from occurring in your business, but you can certainly reduce the probability. By maintaining high standards in the workplace, you can reduce the risk of these events occurring and therefore lessen the likelihood of claims being made against you. Your insurance broker or the insurer themselves can be an excellent resource in advising you on the various ways to reduce the risk of loss. These professionals deal with insurance claims on a daily basis and are able to offer you the benefit of their knowledge and experience in reducing your risk. For a small investment of your time and effort (and that of your employees) you can reduce risk by implementing the following strategies.

Safety monitors

Appoint key people within your business to oversee workplace safety and security. Encourage the more experienced staff to lead by example and to pass on their knowledge to other employees.

Regular repairs

If it's broke, leave nothing to chance and fix it immediately. Have specialist repairs (plumbing and electrical works) carried out by qualified tradespeople.

Overhaul equipment

Regular and planned maintenance of plant and equipment is a must. Have a maintenance schedule set down in writing.

Valuables

Bank money straight away and advise employees and customers to take due care if leaving valuables on your premises.

Emergency equipment

Do you have first aid kits, fire extinguishers, security alarms, fire exits and the like? Do you have enough of them and do they work? Do your employees know where they are kept and how to use them?

Neat and orderly

Maintain a neat and orderly workplace. Don't leave sharp objects lying around; tape down all electrical and telephone cables so people can't trip over them; remove all rubbish daily; don't block emergency exits.

Stock control

Have systems put in place to manage your stock and prevent theft.

Staff training

Provide occupational health and safety training as part of every new employee's induction program. Run regular fire drills and appoint fire wardens. Conduct information sessions for staff on health and safety issues.

13

ENERGY CONSERVATION

Energy conservation is not only a good thing for the environment—it's also great for the bottom line of your business. And the best news is you don't have to spend big to save big. The strategies covered in this chapter are often neglected by businesses when looking at how to reduce operating expenses, as the potential for savings is not as obvious as in some other areas. The following no-cost and low-cost ideas will help your business reduce energy costs and save money.

Chapter 13

Energy conservation

This chapter covers:

Water

Maintenance

Vehicles

246. Identify savings with an energy audit

If you are serious about saving money on your energy bill, look no further than your energy company. Arrange for a meeting at your premises with company representatives and, if possible, have them conduct an energy audit of your business. In some cases this may be a free service. To discover where energy can be saved, you will first need to identify how much you are currently using, where you are using it and how much it is costing you. The energy company can provide good advice on conserving energy and reducing your monthly power bill.

247. Be energy-efficient

Buy and use energy-efficient products for your business. When buying or replacing computers, photocopiers and other office equipment, compare the energy requirements of the different models. Include energy efficiency as one of the main criteria when choosing the features you need in your new piece of equipment. While the savings might not be felt immediately, most energy-efficient models will provide much larger savings over the long term.

248. Off-peak discount

Are you receiving the relevant discounts on power for all your off-peak usage? Speak to your energy company to see if you are eligible for any rebates and ensure you are getting the discounts you deserve. You should be able to ask for a print-out of your energy consumption and ask for a discount on usage during low periods.

Mark manages a privately owned leisure facility consisting of an Olympic-sized swimming pool and two smaller recreational pools. In an attempt to cut costs, Mark commissioned an energy audit by a local engineering firm and discovered that he was liable to receive a rebate on a portion of his energy bill. The firm contacted the energy company and confirmed that the facility was indeed entitled to a small discount for all power consumed between 1 am and 5 am. At first glance the initial rebate did not seem substantial, but after calculating the reduction over a full twelve months, the savings were in the vicinity of $10 000.

249. Enlist the help of employees

Never underestimate the importance of staff cooperation in saving on energy costs. The actions and efforts of your staff will make or break any savings program you put in place. As with all cost-saving activities, encourage your employees to be energy-conscious. Make sure your employees check all the lights have been turned off in the toilets and storerooms before leaving the premises at the end of the day. To verify the extent of the problem, take a walk around your business premises one night after everyone has gone. Is there any office equipment, machinery or lights that should be turned off? (Don't be misled by computer screen savers—they don't save electricity, because the computer is still running.) You could start an energy-saving campaign within your organisation and offer a reward or prize for the individual or department that saves the most energy. Appoint a single person to be responsible for coordinating the campaign, as this will give your employees more ownership of the program.

250. Then ask your customers to help

Educating your customers too on the importance of energy conservation should not be overlooked. You could send out information to all groups who lease your facilities, requesting them to ensure that they turn off all lights directly after use. Place notices above all light switches and at the main exit of each building as a reminder to users to turn off all the power. And as added motivation, simply tell them they are helping to conserve energy that will assist in preventing an increase in the fees.

251. Get it right the first time round

If you are building or renovating business premises, ensure you install all the relevant energy reduction devices then. It will be significantly cheaper than having to make the changes later on. Incorporate some or all of the suggestions in this chapter.

252. Buy energy-efficient equipment

As well as for general office equipment, prioritise energy efficiency as one of the main purchasing criteria for equipment and machinery specific to your industry. For example, restaurants and cafes can save by buying energy-efficient refrigeration equipment, freezers, stoves and cookers. Manufacturers can opt for more efficient electric motors to be used in fans, pumps, compressors and material processing.

Lighting

Brighten up your day and your bank manager's by keeping lighting costs under control. There are tremendous savings to be had for any business that effectively manages the lighting they use.

253. Switch on for increased savings

Do you know how many light switches control the lighting in your business premises? If there are very few or only one, this may present an opportunity to considerably reduce your lighting bill. In many offices, one central switch activates every ceiling light, including those covering segregated offices and meeting rooms. This means that even when these areas are unoccupied, which is normally the case for most meeting rooms, the lights are still burning and consuming power. This is an absolute waste of energy and money. By providing individual light switches for specific areas within your office, retail outlet, factory or workshop, you can more effectively control your lighting and lighting bill.

Peter manages my local indoor basketball centre and he came up with a simple idea to save on lighting costs with the flick of a switch. During quiet times, there would often be only four to six teenagers in the centre playing a game of pick up and using only half the basketball court—yet the lighting for the entire two courts had to be turned on as it was all controlled by one master switch. Peter called in a qualified electrician and changed the configuration so that four switches controlled the lighting for both courts. Each switch operated the lighting for one half of the court. By making this simple change, Peter made considerable savings on his lighting costs.

254. Lighting doesn't have to cost a fortune

Believe it or not, lighting is both the largest user of electricity in most businesses and the easiest area in which to save energy costs. By using a combination of good old common sense and energy-efficient equipment, you can significantly lower your lighting bill. The following ideas will shed some light on how to keep lighting costs to a minimum.

Use energy-efficient bulbs

Replace old light bulbs with energy-efficient ones. Energy-efficient fluorescents use far less wattage than standard fluorescents and last just as long. Although they are more expensive than the standard ones, the energy savings will more than compensate for the extra costs.

Reduce lighting

Remove one fluorescent tube from each two-set fixture that is not situated over desks or work areas. Take half of the light bulbs out of your hallways or remove ceiling lights where there is more lighting than necessary.

Use sensors

Connect occupancy sensors or timers in rooms that are used intermittently. These devices are particularly useful for rooms where people are likely to forget to turn off lights, such as storerooms, toilets, private offices and meeting rooms. Sensors can also be used for external security lighting.

Increase lighting effectiveness

Don't use dark, heavy lampshades and lighting fixtures that absorb light. As an alternative, use reflective surfaces to increase the effectiveness of your lights by reflecting additional light on to the work area.

Keep lights clean

Clean dust, dirt and grease from light bulbs, lenses, fluorescent tubes, lampshades, lighting covers and reflecting surfaces at least twice a year. Make this part of your cleaning/maintenance schedule. Dirty surfaces reduce light output, so cleaning them will increase the brightness of your workspace. This may also allow you to remove some lights or install lower wattage ones, further reducing costs.

Use task lighting

Task lighting provides specific and uniform light to the areas where you actually need light, rather than the entire room. Use lower wattage task lights for close work at desks and work areas to provide light where it is needed; this allows a decrease in general ceiling lighting. Examples of task lights include desk lamps and ceiling downlights.

Paint in light colours

Paint your office and work areas in light colours to gain maximum reflectivity.

Install long life bulbs

Use long life bulbs for hard to reach places. These lights are often found in warehouses, sports stadiums and other buildings with high ceilings where replacing them is a major and costly undertaking.

Reduce wattage

Only use as much wattage as you need. Why use a 100-watt bulb when 60 watts will more than suffice?

Use dimmer switches

Dimmer switches can help reduce wastage by allowing the lighting level to be altered according to the requirements of those using the room.

255. Reduce lighting costs naturally

To conserve energy and reduce your power bill, use as much natural lighting as possible in your business. Here are a few ideas that can be put into action straight away. This is the best source of light and it's free.

- Move office desks and work areas nearer to windows.

- Prune back trees that may be shading windows.

- If you're building or renovating, consider the positioning of the sun so you can take full advantage of natural light.

- Use skylights in areas such as toilets, storerooms, stockrooms and lobby areas.

- Keep the external part of windows clean. It's amazing how much more light gets in through clean windows.

Remove any filing cabinets, cupboards, bookshelves or indoor plants that may be partially or completely covering windows and preventing the maximum amount of sunlight from entering. And take down any posters, photographs, memos or other bits and pieces your employees have stuck on the window closest to them.

Heating and cooling

A comfortable place of work is essential to maintaining a high level of productivity. Your employees cannot perform at their best if your business is too hot or too cold. However, providing the ideal environment can come at great expense. These tips will help you keep those costs in check.

256. Stop leaks and start saving

Is your place of business like a block of Swiss cheese? Are there holes, cracks, crevices, open doorways and windows that make any attempt to heat or cool it result in a hefty power bill? If so then one of the quickest and easiest ways to dramatically reduce that power bill is to close up the spaces where warm/cool air can escape and cool/warm air can enter. To prevent leakage and reduce your energy bill:

■ Check to make sure all windows close properly—best done during windy periods when it is easier to find potential leaks. Repair any problems immediately.

■ Replace any broken or cracked glass in windows.

■ Seal up leaks on both the exterior and interior of your business.

■ Install automatic door closers or electronic sliding doors to guarantee you'll never have a door left open again. This is particularly important for exterior doors.

■ Ensure the space around your airconditioning unit is properly sealed.

■ Place an exterior insulating cover on any window-mounted or above-door airconditioning units during winter.

- Use door snakes to prevent air escaping under your door. These long pieces of material filled with material, dried peas or sand are jammed up against the gap at the base of a door, and go a long way to preventing leakage.

257. Using the sun to save on heating costs

Many businesses are reaping huge savings in heating costs by designing their workplaces to maximise the use of natural sunlight to create a warm and comfortable environment. To warm up your business, use as much glass as possible. Floor to ceiling windows allow the maximum amount of sunlight and warmth into your building. Also, remove window awnings during winter months and keep blinds and shutters open.

Sometimes physical or structural changes are not necessary to take advantage of the sun's heating abilities.

Gerry and Annette own a bed and breakfast in a popular coastal resort. During the quieter winter months, guests are given the north- and east-facing rooms first to take advantage of any sunshine. These rooms are warmer than the other rooms in the complex and therefore require less heating. This simple strategy has been very successful in reducing Gerry and Annette's heating costs.

258. Losing the sun to save on airconditioning costs

Conversely, direct sunlight streaming into the building during the summer months will substantially increase your airconditioning costs. To avoid this:

- Paint the outside of your building using light colours to reflect direct sunlight away from your building.

- Cover windows with awnings, blinds or consider having them tinted.

- Plant deciduous trees in front of windows. These will provide much needed shade in summer and allow in sunlight during winter.

259. Seal off unused spaces

Your place of business may have areas that are never used and may not require heating or airconditioning, such as unused office space, storage areas, ablution facilities and meeting rooms. If possible, seal off these areas by closing heating and cooling vents, keeping doors closed and covering exterior windows.

Louise sublet the three offices adjacent to her own in her single storey office building. Unfortunately, the tenant moved out when their lease expired and Louise was unable to find a replacement. One day she went for a walk through the offices and realised that the airconditioning was still operating, cooling the vacant space. As the windows had no blinds, she bought some black cardboard and taped it over them. She used thicker cardboard to tape over the airconditioning vents in the ceiling and kept the doors shut. She noticed the temperature of her own office instantly becoming cooler. As a result, Louise was able to improve the efficiency of her airconditioning and reduce the cost of keeping her office cool.

260. Use computers to help you save

For larger operations, you may wish to consider installing computerised energy management systems in your business. By supplying heating and cooling only when required, you can reduce energy costs significantly.

Rodney manages an eleven-storey office building in the city. In an attempt to save costs, the owners contacted Rodney and instructed him to reduce the building's energy expenses. Over the following three weeks Rodney surveyed all tenants to determine at what times they arrived in the morning and left in the evening. He quickly discovered that most tenants didn't get in until 8.30 am and most had left by 6 pm. Currently the generators operating the centralised airconditioning would automatically switch on at 7.30 am and turn off at 6.30 pm. By adjusting the operating times in accordance with his research, Rodney saved 7½ hours of running time for his generators per week. Continued observation revealed that most tenants had left by 5.30 pm on a Friday, so Rodney further altered the operating times to save an extra half hour every week. In total, he was able to save 416 hours in annual running costs.

By keeping operating times to a minimum, energy management systems also prolong the life of your equipment.

261. Some more tips to save on airconditioning costs

Airconditioners can really blow out your energy bill if not managed properly. These simple tips maximise the efficiency of your airconditioning while minimising the cost.

■ Make sure the thermostat is working efficiently. Its reading may be inaccurate, so have someone come in and test it.

■ Install your airconditioning unit in the coolest part of the room. Where possible, avoid placing it next to large windows or direct sunlight.

■ Keep the unit's filter, condenser and other parts clean to improve efficiency and output and save you money.

■ Airconditioned rooms should be well protected from direct sunlight.

■ Keep the doors and windows to airconditioned rooms closed at all times. Only open them when necessary.

262. Don't blow your energy savings with fans

As an alternative to installing airconditioning in your business, the humble fan can keep you and your employees cool without the hefty price tag.

■ Turn off all fans when not in use.

■ Set fans on low speed.

■ Place fans close to the areas needing cooling so the speed can be kept on low.

■ Lock the oscillator when a fan is needed in one area, so that air is blown directly to where it is required.

263. Hot and cold savings

Here are a few more ideas you can implement to reduce both heating and cooling costs.

■ Open windows during moderate periods to let out warm air and admit cooler outside air. By keeping windows open at night (if viable in terms of security), you may be able to cool your office for the next day.

- Replace dirty air filters promptly to make it easier for your airconditioning system to work more efficiently. Clean filters, fans and motors to prolong their life.

- Ensure external doors and window frames have good weather stripping. Enclose the areas surrounding window airconditioners, as this open space allows the cool air to escape.

- As previously mentioned, use door snakes to seal the gaps at the bottom of doors. These are very effective in keeping warm air in and cold air out.

- Ensure that furniture, indoor plants and paintings do not obstruct heaters, radiators and air intakes and vents.

- Insulate and shield windows well, since they are the most heat-conductive part of any building. Closed curtains, shades and blinds will keep out the heat in summer and keep in the warmth in winter. Open them on sunny days to enjoy some free solar heating. Consider additional shielding options such as awnings, fixed lattice grills, recessed windows and shade trees.

- Lower the heating thermostat by one degree a week to determine how low the setting can comfortably be; alternatively, raise the airconditioning by one degree a week to determine how high it can comfortably be. This is particularly effective in space where people are relatively inactive, perhaps sitting at desks or behind counters most of the time.

- Many factories and warehouses have large ventilation grilles to allow air to flow through during the warmer months. Cover these during winter to prevent warm air escaping and cold air entering.

- If you run a motel or bed and breakfast, provide extra blankets in winter.

Water

264. Save water and save money

Regardless of whether your business consumes large quantities of water, every single drop has an impact. These tips can lead to worthwhile savings.

- Reduce the hot water temperature on your water heater thermostats to reflect the usage. The temperature can be reduced on thermostats controlling shower and toilet facilities as the water doesn't need to be extremely hot.

- Only run washing machines and dishwashers with full loads.

- If you operate a hostel, motel or hotel, only change the bed linen and towels on the request of guests staying multiple nights.

- If you haven't done so already, alter your toilet cisterns to provide both full and economy flush, and fit timers to urinal auto-flush systems.

- Immediately repair any leaking taps or water pipes.

- Do not leave the hose running while washing company vehicles. If possible, don't wash them as often.

- Protect yourself against burst pipes by installing pressure-sensitive valves that will cut off the water supply.

265. Heat your water with the sun

Many small businesses such as fitness centres, restaurants, drycleaners and motels have a large demand for water heating. This can be economically and reliably met by solar energy. If it's good enough for domestic use, there should be no reason why your business can't benefit from it.

Maintenance

An effective maintenance program for your business has far-reaching effects. Besides increasing the life expectancy of your assets, well-maintained facilities and services can prevent accidents, thereby reducing insurance costs. Properly maintained equipment also operates more efficiently and is cheaper to run. Here are some ways to help you maintain a tight control on maintenance expenses.

266. Prevention is better than cure

It's difficult to accurately measure the savings made through preventative maintenance programs. However, when you consider the consequences of a major breakdown in machinery or equipment, the cost of regularly maintaining your assets is a small price to pay.

Andre operated a preventative maintenance program for his fleet of courier vans, and had to replace his vehicles when they were ten years old and had clocked over 400 000 kilometres. A competitor who had not used a maintenance program needed to replace his vehicles when they were five years old and had done only 150 000 kilometres.

267. Stagger your maintenance programs

Building and machinery maintenance can put a strain on your business's bottom line. Postponing non-essential maintenance tasks will offer a certain level of relief; however, putting these off for too long can cause excessive repair or replacement costs. Rather than neglect maintenance issues due to a lack of funds, take a more planned approach and simply reduce the number of times maintenance is performed in certain areas.

Gerard slashed the maintenance costs of his shopping centre by reducing the frequency that many of the maintenance tasks were undertaken. Here are just some of the changes he made.

■ The internal potted plants were changed twice a year instead of three times.

■ External lines and directional road markings were repainted three instead of four times a year.

■ Car park markings were repainted annually rather than every six months.

■ Hardier trees and bushes were planted as they required less watering.

■ Pruning was cut back to twice a year.

- Grassed areas were not cut so short, requiring less watering.

- Light fittings were cleaned every six months rather than quarterly.

- Common floor areas were polished once every ten days instead of every seven days.

Consider staggering major maintenance requirements so that they do not fall within the same time period. Develop your implementation plan around the amount of money you will have available for these purposes.

268. Major maintenance shouldn't lose you business

Try to schedule major maintenance activities during down time to avoid disruption to your services, loss of customers and therefore loss of revenue. Having customers walk through a partial construction site is also tempting fate as far as injuries are concerned. For instance, outdoor swimming pools carry out major maintenance on the pool, pumps and filtration systems during the winter months when the business is closed. My local basketball centre closes for a week between Christmas and New Year to resurface the playing courts.

269. Graffiti can cost you a fortune

You only need to take a ride on the train to see the ugly and expensive effects graffiti has on many businesses. There are a number of products on the market to seal external walls, so that if paint is applied removing it becomes a fairly easy exercise. The downside is the cost of these products—you will need to weigh up the cost of having your premises sealed against the likelihood that they will become a victim of graffiti. The following are far cheaper alternatives that can be implemented immediately.

- Increase security lighting to the external areas of your business.

- Repaint walls that have been tagged as soon as possible.

- Grow shrubs, trees and creepers to cover external walls.

- Place latticework in front of walls.

If your business is unfortunate enough to be tagged, take photos of the graffiti and report the incident to the police. They may be able to identify the perpetrator from the distinctly individual tag left on the wall of your building.

Offenders who are caught are often made to make restitution to owners of the defiled premises.

Vehicles

Vehicle costs can be a large drain on company expenses. Apart from the initial cost of purchasing vehicles, there are also the considerable ongoing maintenance and running costs. Keep your vehicle running costs to a minimum with the following suggestions.

270. Use alternative fuel sources to save

If your business maintains a fleet of vehicles, consider how alternative fuel sources such as natural gas, propane, ethanol, methanol and electricity can possibly save you money. Plumbing and electrical contractors, florists, couriers, office suppliers, drycleaners and caterers are all candidates for fuel savings.

Joe drives his own taxi and a few years ago he converted his business on wheels to natural gas. His taxi clocks up thousands of kilometres each month and he has predicted savings of around 15 per cent on fuel costs by changing to natural gas. With the increase in petrol prices, Joe's savings have undoubtedly increased even further.

271. Cut costs while travelling around at work

The simple act of travelling to and from your place of business, attending meetings, visiting clients, making deliveries and picking up stock can ultimately cost your business a great deal of money over the course of a year. Consider the cost of parking—perhaps you are paying hundreds of dollars per month for just one secure parking space in the city. In other cases, many businesses spend tens of thousands of dollars on building and maintaining car parks for their staff and customers. Incorporate the following alternatives into your business and slash transport overheads at the same time.

Public transport

Do you or your staff really need to drive to work, only to have the car sit in a parking bay all day long? Consider using public transport to travel to and from work. Where possible, use public transport to get to and from your appointments. It may be just as quick catching a bus or train as driving; it is certainly a lot cheaper and you don't have to pay for parking or spend time looking for a parking place. I try and use public transport as much as I can for these reasons, and I use the travelling time to prepare for a meeting or go over some notes.

Car pool to save costs

When you and an employee need to attend a meeting, use only one car, and request that your staff do likewise. Taking two cars means doubling up on fuel and car parking. Apart from saving costs, you can use the travel time wisely to prepare your game plan for the meeting and go over briefing notes.

On your bike

I heard of one medium-sized business that offered its top executives the option of a free membership to the nearby fitness centre in lieu of free parking. As many of the managers lived within a thirty-minute cycle from the office, the owner calculated that it would be cheaper and healthier for the business to pay for gym membership so employees could shower and change after riding to work, than it would be to pay for parking. Half of the managers took up the offer, saving the company around $4000 a year in parking fees (and no doubt improving the managers' fitness and energy levels).

Pool vehicles

Many businesses feel compelled to provide a full-time company vehicle to employees who do a modest amount of travelling. Certainly, for some positions having a vehicle is an integral part of the overall package. In other cases, consider maintaining a small pool of company vehicles that employees can check out during the day when they need to attend to business matters away from the office.

Look after company vehicles

Operate your vehicles efficiently and train employees to have the same respect for company vehicles as they would for their own car. By maintaining vehicles regularly you will reduce wear and tear and the likelihood of costly breakdowns occurring. And to get the most mileage from a tank of petrol, ensure you keep all tyres properly inflated, remove any unnecessary weight, clean the filters and have the vehicle serviced regularly.

Promote proper driving

Make it a policy of the business that all speeding fines incurred, even when driving a company vehicle, are to be paid by the respective employee. Careless and inconsiderate driving can also result in motor accidents, incurring your business additional costs from increased insurance premiums, payments and repairs, so promote careful driving among your employees. Here are some ways to do so.

- Conduct an education campaign with staff on correct driving techniques.

- Have your vehicle insurer or vehicle licensing department conduct a written road safety test for all your staff—you can make this a lot of fun but maintain the serious message.

- Put a chart on the staff noticeboard indicating the number of days since the last vehicle accident.

- Make staff liable for any fines or summonses they receive as a result of poor driving.

- Include a safe driving 'tip of the month' in your staff newsletter.

- Include company standards and expectations regarding safe driving as an addendum to all job descriptions and in all staff manuals.

- Promote the 'Big 4' safe driving practices—wear a seatbelt at all times; never drive under the influence of alcohol or drugs; don't speed; don't use a mobile phone while driving.

For many employees, a compulsory component of their job is that they hold a current and valid driver's licence. Make these members of staff aware that if they lose their licence, they stand a chance of losing their job. It's as simple as that.

Confirm all appointments

Call (or ask your secretary to) before you leave for an appointment to make sure it is still going ahead. Sometimes appointments will not eventuate because people forget, get called away on urgent business, fall ill or are away from work for the day. There is nothing more frustrating than turning up to an appointment only to be told the person is not available and you will have to reschedule.

You be the host

Given the choice, I will always try to host any meetings or appointments at my place of business. In doing so, I avoid spending time and money on transport and parking, I am not away from the office which means I can get more work done, and if by chance the meeting needs to be cancelled at the last minute I am not greatly inconvenienced.

272. Have employees use their own car

Providing company cars for some employees can be a very expensive exercise. It may be more sensible to have employees use their own cars and reimburse them for work-related mileage. Just scan the employment section of the newspaper for adverts with the words 'own vehicle essential' and you will see how more and more businesses are moving towards this arrangement.

As an alternative, some companies are now providing motorbikes instead of a car. For instance, many courier companies are increasing the number of motorcycles they use instead of the traditional delivery vans. Motorcycles have many advantages, including:

- They cost far less to buy or lease and to run than a car.

- They can slice through city traffic and avoid traffic snarls, saving considerable time.

- You can enhance your business's image with a fleet of motorbikes buzzing around the city.

GENERAL COST-SAVING IDEAS

Just when you thought you had all the information you needed to slash the operating costs of your business, here are some more suggestions to save you a few extra dollars.

Chapter 14

General cost-saving ideas

This chapter covers:

273. Save on subscriptions to magazines, journals and professional organisations

Review your magazine and newspaper subscriptions. Are they all necessary or can you cancel some of them? I have worked in organisations that have multiple subscriptions to the same publication and I know from experience that half of them weren't even read. So only order one copy and circulate magazines and newspapers among your employees. If your budget permits, take out a multiyear subscription, as the individual cost per copy becomes significantly cheaper. Alternatively, get the information you need from sources such as the Internet or your public library—both free.

Professional organisations are also an area where many businesses can save. There is a virtual smorgasbord of business associations and networking groups your business can become involved with. Review each and every membership carefully and write down the benefits of belonging. Retain those organisations that give you direct benefits and pull out of those that don't give you what you need. Can you change your membership status to save money? Most organisations have different membership types including associate, full, student and individual or company member. Some categories are cheaper than others, yet provide much the same benefits.

274. Use professional associations to save

Take full advantage of those professional associations you do decide to join and get the most from the membership fee you pay. Many associations offer a wide range of benefits for members, such as group insurance deals, free professional advice, networking opportunities and supplier discounts.

275. Donations

Every business wants to be a good corporate citizen and contribute in a meaningful way to charitable organisations and community projects. Many see it is a responsibility. However, if your business really can't afford to provide assistance then don't. When business improves and you are financially stable, you can resume donations.

Andy owned the corner hardware store and was a regular sponsor of the local football club and many other community projects.

> Recently a large hardware chain had opened up nearby and Andy had noticed a reduction in business. Despite this setback, Andy was still committed to sponsoring the football club but withdrew his assistance from the other events.

276. Christmas and other seasonal staff parties

Gone are the days when it was the company's responsibility to put on a free Christmas party for employees and their families. The best company functions I have attended have been good fun and great for morale—but have also been very simple and affordable affairs.

> *Stuart's company held a Christmas party for one hundred employees and their families. A barbeque was held at a nearby park with plenty of food and drink for everyone. Management organised a program of games and activities for the children and their parents and it was these events that proved the biggest hit. Finally Santa Claus appeared with a sack bulging with sweets and other goodies. The day was a huge success and employees were still talking about it well into the new year. The simplest things in life are often the best.*

Many businesses have established staff social clubs whereby employees contribute a small amount of money each week. At the end of the year a sizeable sum has been collected and the club committee sets about organising an end-of-year function. The company also makes a contribution towards the event, but it is nowhere near as much as if they had to pay for everything alone. Does your business have a social club? If not, then get one started. They are great for morale and easy on your bottom line.

277. Charge back expenses to clients

Recoup some of the costs of doing business with your customers by charging for everything. Professional service providers such as real estate agents, lawyers and psychologists do this all the time. Doctors also do it—most general practitioners charge a flat rate for a consultation. If they are required to do extra tests or provide additional services, they will charge you accordingly. It can work for just about any business. When you incur expenses that aren't a regular part of providing your product or service, charge your client or figure the additional costs into their bills. A good example of charging expenses to clients is that of tenants who lease space within a serviced office building. In addition to their monthly rental, they pay for any extra services they require from the management, such as use of meeting facilities, typing, emails, faxing, shredding documents, taking messages and organising couriers.

278. Collection of refuse

Many businesses pay for large dumpsters to store their rubbish in addition to the refuse collection services provided by their local government authority. Keep your collection costs down by recycling, reusing and giving away whatever you can.

- As paper makes up a large portion of rubbish disposed of by most businesses, contact your local recycling company and they will come and collect your recyclable paper for free.

- Share the costs of collection bins with a neighbouring business.

- Does your business produce waste that can be used by another business? Sell it to them or give it away—either way, it won't cost you anything to get rid of it. A local gardening centre offered to remove all the old pieces of brick, tile and wood from a builders' construction site. They crushed the bricks and tile into rubble for use in garden landscaping while the wood was turned into low-cost pot stands and garden benches.

- Don't let the refuse company empty your dumpster until it is full, especially if you are charged every time it is emptied.

279. More recycling ideas to save you money

The benefits recycling can have for your business is only determined by the creativity of you and your staff.

- Reuse envelopes to send out invoices and payments.

- Shred paper and use it as packing fill, or reuse those styrofoam peanuts suppliers have put in their deliveries to your business.

- Use incoming boxes and recycle them to send products to customers

- Encourage employees to bring in their own glasses and coffee mugs, rather than buying plastic cups.

- Use rechargeable batteries for torches, two-way radios and other battery-operated pieces of equipment.

- One hotel recycled their stained and torn king and queen-size bed sheets and converted them into single bed sheets. Bath towels were cut into hand towels and old linen was used as cleaning rags.

- Fran's cleaning business uses refillable pump-spray bottles rather than aerosol cans for their cleaning chemicals.

280. Eliminate food at meetings

Have you ever been to a meeting where the host provides sandwiches and pastries that don't end up getting eaten? I have. People are too shy, in too much of a hurry, too fussy or just want to focus on the business at hand. What happens is the staff end up taking it home. One day my wife came home with a whole chocolate cake that was bought earlier in the day for a meeting of her company's senior management, but was never touched. Coffee and tea is probably as far as you need to go.

281. Get the news for free

Does your business have the newspaper delivered daily? Why not hook up to the net and read the news on-line. You can read any major newspaper and you don't have to worry about paying for it or disposing of the paper when you've finished with it. Or do what my good friend Shane does and read the paper for free while enjoying a cup of coffee at his favourite cafe. One cafe I go to even sells the daily paper for only 50c with any tea or coffee purchased.

282. Plastic shopping bags

Get your staff to bring in those plastic shopping bags that every household accumulates by the hundreds. Use these as office bin liners—they will save you a great deal on buying garbage bags, not to mention stop your bins from getting dirty and smelly from all the rubbish, food and the like that find their way into the average office bin.

283. Every office has a green thumb

Plants are an excellent addition to any office or work environment but they can also prove to be expensive. If you are currently renting plants for your office, I would suggest finding out if any employee is keen on gardening, and nominate them the main supplier and maintainer of your new batch of office plants. Ask them to bring in some plants from home and offer to pay them a small fee for them. I've done this on a number of occasions and it has given a great sense of responsibility to the employee concerned and everyone gets involved. And it only costs you a few bucks for the plants.

284. Take the plunge and save

If you are brave enough to roll up your sleeves and delve into those recycling bins, you could end up saving your business a small fortune in stationery items.

John's office is located on the third floor of a serviced office complex. On each floor is a small kitchen, photocopy room and paper recycling bin. Being a serviced office, there are many short-term tenants coming and going and the bin is often overflowing with rubbish. Every evening John spends five minutes sorting through the contents of the bin and salvaging everything—reusable paper, boxes of envelopes, manila folders, pens, paperclips, file dividers, bulldog clips, plastic sleeves and even the occasional lever arch file. John calculates he has saved over $1500 in eighteen months on his office stationery bill.

Remember, one man's junk is another man's treasure. If you see people throwing stuff out, do the right thing and help them by taking it off their hands. And don't worry about what they'll think—just consider the money you are saving.

285. Low-cost research

Many businesses spend tens of thousands of dollars conducting intensive customer research to identify the needs and wants of their customers.

This information can be put to very good use in developing new products and services, evaluating the effectiveness of marketing strategies, identifying new markets and opportunities, and formulating winning customer service ideas. But market research doesn't have to be a major expense. Here are some effective research methods that won't break the bank.

Students

As previously mentioned, there are many university students who can assist you with your research needs at little or no cost to you.

Talk to your customers

There's nothing like getting information straight from the horse's mouth. It's amazing what you can find out by having a casual chat with your customers. Some of the best cost-saving, revenue-generating and customer service ideas have come from my customers.

Comment forms

Some of your customers won't feel comfortable speaking their mind in person; however, they may be happy to put their thoughts and ideas in writing. Design a simple form to be left in a spot visible to your customers. You may even include one when mailing out invoices or payments.

Survey on sales forms

Include a small survey on your sales or registration form. Ask one or two pertinent questions that will give you an insight into the needs of your customers.

Let someone else do it for you

If you're not concerned about being the market leader, then sit back and let your competition do all the research for you. Wait for them to release their latest product or service and then copy it. They have probably conducted a lot of their own research to help shape their latest promotion.

Read trade journals and other relevant publications

These are normally packed full of information on the latest trends and ideas. Try to get hold of publications from other countries, as these will often provide information not yet in place in your market.

FINALLY, MANAGING YOUR EXPENSES FOR PROFIT

The effective management of small business overheads is not a case of 'pinching pennies to save pounds'. Yes, big profits can be made from a multitude of small savings; however, you don't have to be stingy in order to profit from your savings. On the contrary, the aim of any successful small business operator should be to maximise their existing resources, develop intelligent spending behaviour and reduce potential waste and loss. The ideas in this chapter should help you do just that.

Chapter 15

Finally, managing your expenses for profit

This chapter covers:

307. Communicate with your staff regularly

308. Target insignificant expenses first

309. Every business needs a scrooge

310. Ego has a price

311. No frills cuts your bills

312. Price increases cost you money

313. A penny saved is a penny earned

286. Develop a balanced profit mentality

Never, never, never forget the main reason your business exists—to make money. Sometimes as business managers we get so caught up in daily challenges and activities that we lose focus of this first and most imperative goal. It is essential that you develop a profit mentality within your business and ensure every member of your operation is focused on making profits the correct way. And what is the correct way?

Profit is what you have left over once you have subtracted all your expenses from money earned (revenue minus expenses). Therefore, to maximise profits you must take a balanced approach towards making the most amount of money in the most cost-effective way. There is no sense in generating huge revenue if your costs are enormous. Alternatively, a business will not last very long if they are doing a great job at reducing operating overheads but are losing sight of making sales. Increasing revenue and reducing expenses are of equal importance, so treat them as such. Expense is a natural part of any business and should therefore be treated with respect as opposed to fear. Revenue and expenses are the yin and yang of any successful business. It is virtually impossible to have one without the other. By incurring expenses you must also be generating revenue for your business; if money is *not* coming in then you're running a welfare program, not a business. Accept expenses as an occupational hazard and aim to minimise your overheads while maximising your revenue.

287. Big savings come in small packages

Some people put aside a small amount of their pay packet into a savings account, so that over the course of twelve months that small contribution grows into a substantial sum. You can use the same approach in your business to great effect. By reducing your total business overheads by only one hundred dollars a week you will ultimately save around $5200 a year. So do you think you can find one hundred dollars worth of savings a week or more? Small savings over time can grow into big profits, so start saving now.

288. Mothers are the best savers

When my three sisters and I were growing up, we never seemed to go without anything—yet we were certainly not rich by any stretch of the imagination. My father was a corporal in the army and my mother worked part-time in a delicatessen. So how did they manage to do it?

Well, my mother knew exactly how much money she had to spend each fortnight with the money she and my father brought in (their revenue). She then deducted regular bills (her fixed costs) and savings (their profit). What was left over was used for food, entertainment and spending on us (her variable costs). If she needed more money because of unforeseen costs (e.g. one of us needed new sports gear or had a school camp coming up), she had two options. She could either get a few extra hours work to increase her pay, which wasn't always possible, or she could cut back spending on her 'variable expenses' and make that extra money go further.

Your business can easily do the same. In many businesses it is difficult to manage a consistent level of sales (revenue) week after week. However, one thing you can control is your overheads. If the sales aren't rolling in then have a look at how you can reduce your variable expenditure or make the money you have go even further.

289. Ask your employees

Your staff can be the single best source of ideas for saving your business thousands of dollars. Remember, they are in the front line of your operations. They deal with customers, suppliers and contractors every day, they manufacture your products, and they manage the administration of the business. Often we don't give our staff enough credit—or opportunity—for the positive contributions they can make to our business. You should aim to create an environment where your employees are encouraged to put forward suggestions on how to reduce expenses for your business.

It is also important that you respond to and act on all suggestions. If an idea cannot be implemented, let the staff member know why. They may eventually come back with an even better idea. For suggestions that are accepted, make sure that the employee plays a significant role in the implementation and that they are rewarded.

290. Let employees enjoy the spoils of success

'What's in it for me?' The cornerstone of any successful sales and marketing strategy is to identify and convey the benefit your product or service will have for your prospect. If you really want your staff to support your cost-saving endeavours, show them how they will benefit from doing so.

Recently, the leadership at an equipment and machinery hire company shared around one million dollars in profits with their staff. Earlier in the year the management had informed staff that things weren't going as budgeted. They got the staff involved in a wide range of cost-saving strategies and used the sharing of profits as a carrot. This bright idea was a huge success, with some staff receiving up to $2000 as a bonus.

If your employees feel they are truly part of the decision-making process and they will gain if cost-saving targets are achieved, then they will be more motivated to achieve these goals.

291. Get a real job

An excellent way to evaluate your processes is to spend time working side by side with your employees. By spending a day or two doing their job with them, you will gain a far better understanding of what they do and the processes they undertake. Some of the biggest corporations in the world have 'swap a job' as a regular part of their operations.

When I managed a call centre for an international hospitality company, I spent two days with my data entry staff learning everything there was to learn about their job, including having to enter 500 sales leads into the database. Despite numb fingers (I'm not a great typist), I discovered my employees were entering a lot of irrelevant data the sales consultants didn't require. By changing the essential information required, data entry staff were able to increase the number of leads entered by a massive 300 per day or 75 000 per year.

292. Target one expense at a time

One method I have successfully used for managing expenses has been to select one specific item, accumulate all the information about its current situation, brainstorm possible changes and then put them into practice.

One of the main costs for a telemarketing call centre is the telephones (see Chapter 6). After receiving a huge bill one month, I pored over the itemised account looking for opportunities for savings.

The first thing that hit me was the high proportion of calls made to mobile phones and long-distance numbers. I also noticed that there were four telephone lines from which no calls were made. It turned out these lines were not being used but we were still paying rental on them. They were quickly disconnected and other lines were barred to prevent mobile and STD calls being made. We also altered the sourcing and distribution of our leads so that consultants were only given local numbers to call. These strategies resulted in a massive 25 per cent savings in telephone costs. As an added bonus, our sales actually increased, resulting in a further jump in profits.

293. Just say no

I used to have a real problem saying no. In fact my friends used to call me 'Mr Nice Guy' and people occasionally took advantage of my trusting nature. In business you can't afford to have anyone—your staff, a colleague, a supplier, a customer, a family member—take advantage of you. If you have a tough time saying no in business, you could end up with too many overpaid staff, excess inventory, bad service or a poor quality product. The ability to say no to things that don't benefit the bottom line is a critical attribute of every successful small business operator. If it makes sense and looks like it would benefit the business, be sure to consider it. But if you cannot approve the request or idea, then say no and be sure you explain the reasons why. Your strength of character will save your business money and your honesty may just mean they will come back to you with a much better idea.

294. Manage your expenses by walking around

The simple act of walking around your premises, or a competitor's (if possible), can open your eyes to new ways to save.

If ever there was an opportunity to reduce businesses expenses by going for a walk, I had it when I managed a shopping complex that covered over half a million square feet of retail space and six levels of car parking. Cost-saving by walking around the shopping complex became a major part of my day. I would choose a topic such as painting, then call the relevant manager and off we would go.

> *We would divide the mall into sections (car park, concourse, public areas, plant and equipment rooms) and search for opportunities to save costs—opportunities we found in abundance. So turn off your computer and mobile phone, leave your desk and start saving your business some money.*

295. Do away with bureaucracy

I am amazed at some of the cumbersome and protracted procedures many small businesses have in place. There is a big difference between having stringent management procedures that guard against the potential loss of profitability, and surrounding yourself with an endless stream of red tape, costing you time and money. Declare war on excessive forms of bureaucracy like purchasing approvals requiring five separate signatures, three-inch-thick reports and pointless memos that are copied to every member of your staff including the cleaner. You should replace these time and money wasters with effective dialogue, a simple email or a quick phone call.

296. Do things well and do them once

> *Allan works for the local council fixing potholes in the road. He is a perfectionist and lives by the motto, 'If you want something done properly, then do it yourself'. He stays out in the hot sun making sure that every pothole is filled, compacted and sealed correctly. He takes it as a professional insult if a hole he has worked on needs to be repaired again. Allan says, 'When you do something, you make sure you do it right the first time. Then you don't have to waste time and money having to go back and do it all over again. After all, I've got plenty of other holes that need fixing.'*

Enough said. Remember, you have only one chance to make a first impression. If it isn't good, that customer probably won't come back again. If you send the wrong order, everything must be repackaged and sent out again. If your product has a defect, it must be replaced. If you order too much stock, you can't send it back. The message is clear. Do things right the first time round and save.

297. Take a step back from your business

It's far too easy to get caught up in the daily grind of running a business and not see the wood for the trees. And it is often too late when we realise there is a problem with our finances. As small business operators, we must develop the ability to step back and objectively evaluate what is and what isn't working.

I regularly set aside one hour of peace and quiet away from the office each week to sit down and review my budgets and accounts. Sometimes I even take a whole day off to reflect on specific aspects of my business, isolating important issues and attempting to identify potential changes that I can implement to increase my revenue and save money. It's important that when you do take a step back, it is with a specific goal in mind. Don't try and cover too many areas, as you will end up achieving very little. Select one or two areas of your business that you want to focus on and give them your all.

298. If it's broken, fix it straight away

Any problem with your business, big or small, has the potential to become very costly. Lost revenue, increased expenses, employee problems, litigation, lost production time, dissatisfied customers and damaged inventory can all greatly affect your bottom line. The key to how much damage any of these problems can potentially inflict on your business is determined by how you deal with them.

Danny, the manager of a marketing agency that sold dining and accommodation memberships, found himself in a dilemma. While his staff were achieving sales at a level higher than expected, he also found that a large number of members were cancelling their benefits. His sales staff were all very well trained, he had an excellent product and existing customers were extremely satisfied when they actually used their membership. Danny quickly investigated this problem and realised that many of the staff were informing prospects that they could return their package within 14 days and receive a complete refund. As they had nothing to lose, many customers went ahead with the membership, only to return it within the given time period. The downside for the business was the significant expenditure incurred through sales commissions, postage, printing and card embossing costs. As soon as the problem was identified, employees were given alternative strategies not only to close the sale but also to get new members to use their privileges immediately. The result was a continued high level of sales and a marked decrease in cancellations.

Not dealing with problems immediately and in an expedient manner can result in a severe loss of business or even the complete closure of your company. In order to prevent your business losing money, productivity and customers, you must quickly identify problems, find out the cause, develop solutions and implement them straight away. The important thing is to do something—and do it without delay.

299. Manage your business as if times were tough

Smart small business operators run a tight ship regardless of whether times are good or bad. We've all seen it before (and we may even be guilty of it ourselves)—a business experiencing outstanding sales and growth becomes complacent in how they manage the business and control expenses. This complacency results in the decline of their employees' motivation, level of service to their customers, productivity, product quality and, most importantly, their profits. Always keep at the forefront of your mind that things could change overnight. Don't be paranoid, just be prepared. At any time a new competitor can enter the market, the economy can slump, there can be a major change in business conditions (such as the recent hike in public liability insurance) or an industrial relations issue could prevent the delivery of vital raw materials. By being vigilant in your management, you will always be in a much better position to deal with any challenges that arise. If you're not prepared, you can guarantee that one of your competitors will be.

300. How will this affect the rest of my business?

This tip is simple—think first. When reducing your business expenses, always first assess the impact that each specific strategy will have on your business. As a start, consider the following.

Potential return on investment

Are you able to quantify in money or time how great your savings will be for the amount of time, money and other resources you will have to invest? There is no use spending $2000 on some new technology that will return a savings of only $200 per year. It will take more than ten years for you to achieve a return on your initial outlay.

Time and resources required

Just how much money, staff time and other resources will be required to make the intended savings possible? Do you have these resources available? Be aware of 'opportunity costs'. It is not worth spending two hours to go and pick up a new piece of equipment yourself in order to save the $100 delivery fee when you could have been spending that time prospecting for new business or developing a new revenue-generating sales strategy.

Impact on your product and service quality

There is no point implementing cost-saving measures if they have a negative effect on your product or your service. A friend's company used to send products to their customers by overnight courier. As a cost-cutting measure, they changed their procedures to a slower delivery time. While this saved them a lot of money, they also lost a lot of customers to their competitors who were still offering the overnight service.

Management support

As owner and operator of your small business, are you 100 per cent behind all cost-saving strategies? Lead from the front and don't think, say or do anything that will contradict these efforts.

Ease of implementation

How long will each strategy take to implement? Can all staff be involved or just one or two people? What resources are required? Is any technical knowledge needed? Is it easy to do? Here's a hint—start with the easy strategies first.

Effect on employees

Establish if employees will be required to do more work and whether this is warranted. Strategies need to have a positive impact on quality, service, productivity and morale. It is your employees who will determine the success of your cost-saving strategies, so give them a reason to make them work.

Alignment with your organisation's goals

Are your strategies in sync with your business goals? If your aim is to provide the fastest and most reliable delivery service out of all of your competitors, there is no point opting for a slower delivery method in order to save costs.

Political correctness

A major telecommunications company was recently involved in a publicity stunt that was going to reap them plenty of high-range publicity for literally nothing. It involved an international rugby union match and a streaker with the company's logos emblazoned across his naked body. The company received a tremendous amount of publicity but the general public, media and authorities frowned upon the stunt.

Possible future implications

Think ahead! What could the implications be in a month, six months, one year or even ten years? Cutting staffing levels will definitely save you money in the short term, but what effect will it have on your business in six to twelve months?

Too often, a business will implement a cost-saving measure only for it to have a negative and costly impact in another area. It is crucial to consider all the consequences of your strategies (use the points outlined above as a guide). If you fail to do so, your biggest enemy will become a lack of customers, which no amount of cost saving can help you overcome.

301. The 10 per cent approach

In an attempt to become more profitable, many businesses make the mistake of cutting their expenses too drastically. Laying off a large portion of one's work force is an all too common example of this. Such stringent measures generally have a more negative impact on the business than the intended savings. It is better to aim for smaller, incremental savings over time; a 10 per cent reduction, for example, has worked very well for me in the past. Look at each expense item and determine how much is required, in dollar terms, to achieve a 10 per cent reduction, then look at devising strategies that will enable you to best achieve this. Once again, ask yourself what impact these strategies will have on your business.

302. What is everyone else doing?

Your daily and community newspapers, small business magazines, industry newsletters, trade associations and service groups can provide you with a wealth of ideas on innovative cost-saving strategies successfully implemented by other companies. Why reinvent the wheel when you can apply someone else's smart ideas to your business? I hope you will do likewise with the tried and tested ideas presented in this book.

303. 'That's the way we've always done it!'

Resistance to change is very common in many businesses. In some instances this mentality permeates the whole organisation, while in others it afflicts only certain employees. Regardless of the extent to which it exists, resistance to change has the potential to severely damage a business. A classic example is a company's inability to embrace technological advances.

When I took over the management of a multistorey shopping complex in 1996, purchase orders, internal memos and other documents were prepared using a typewriter and carbon paper. No one had access to email and receipts were still prepared manually. The company directors took a lot of convincing to supply personal computers to appropriate staff members, but on doing so not only did we see a marked improvement in productivity, staff morale also shot through the roof.

Old habits die hard but failure to embrace change can spell a prolonged and painful death for any business.

304. There's no point flogging a dead horse

All too often businesses try desperately to make a bad decision work. Managers keep pumping resources into the flailing effort and the more they try, the worse things actually get. The successful small business operator knows when to cut their losses by abandoning bad decisions and focusing their energy on more productive and meaningful activities. Sometimes it's a matter of simply swallowing your pride and moving on.

Johnny is a personal trainer and runs his own fitness business. Early mornings and early evenings are his busiest times and he sets prices accordingly to maximise his return. When he started the business, a recurring problem was customers failing to turn up for their appointments without prior notice. This went on for over six months but Johnny did nothing about it, believing the problem would eventually resolve itself. Unfortunately it didn't and he continued to suffer lost income. Finally, out of frustration and disappointment Johnny implemented a system whereby his customers had to give a minimum 24 hours notice, otherwise they would be liable to pay for the session. Not surprisingly, the number of cancellations declined dramatically and when they did occur, Johnny was not out of pocket.

Being stubborn or arrogant will only have a negative impact on your bottom line and could make it difficult, if not impossible, to recover losses.

305. Become very good at negotiating

The ability to negotiate is a critical skill that all business owners and managers should develop. On a daily basis you may be negotiating contracts, leases, supply agreements, product prices, staff salaries and wages. If you don't have the necessary skills to negotiate the best outcome for your business, you are probably losing money. If your negotiation skills are lacking, then buy one of the many good books around or attend a seminar or workshop on effective negotiation skills.

Charlie is the sales manager for a small software company. His company was releasing a new product and Charlie had to arrange a venue for the launch, so he contacted a local hotel and was given a quote for room hire, equipment and catering. He asked for a cheaper rate and in subsequent weeks the hotel sales manager and national sales manager gave him further reductions. If Charlie had stopped to assess the situation, he would have realised that the hotel was desperate for his business and they would have given even further discounts had he pushed them. After all, why would the hotel's national sales manager become actively involved in such a small event for an even smaller business?

Remember, most things are negotiable. The problem is most people don't request a better deal—all you have to do is ask.

306. Set an example

I worked for a five-star hotel chain in Malaysia during the economic crisis of the mid-90s and experienced first-hand the devastating effects a recession can have on a business, its staff and their families. To make matters worse, the country was covered in a thick, choking smog caused by massive plantation fires, leaving the tourism market struggling to stay afloat. While ordinary staff members were doing everything they could to save costs and jobs, including forgoing their end of year bonuses, a senior executive of the company was presented with a brand new Volvo sedan. This was a crucial decision by the senior management that totally demoralised the organisation.

If you are asking your staff to make sacrifices and cut costs, you should lead by example. The 'do as I say, not as I do' attitude can do more harm to your business than any recession.

307. Communicate with your staff regularly

Honesty is the best policy. If you are reducing expenses because your business is going through a tough time, be sure to let all your staff know what is happening, state the reasons why and tell them how they can help. Open, two-way communication is more likely to win understanding and support from employees than the familiar cloak-and-dagger antics undertaken by many companies, whose employees first hear about cost-cutting measures on receiving their termination notice.

Here are some suggestions to get your staff on side.

- Conduct information forums to explain what is happening and why.

- Celebrate successes and keep staff informed of the company's progress.

- Hold strategy meetings to develop ideas on how to make improvements.

- Include rank and file staff in all discussions.

- Have some fun—hold a competition with prizes for the best ideas.

- Place notices on staff bulletin boards.

- Make announcements in staff meetings.

- Have an 'open door' policy so employees feel comfortable to talk to you about their concerns.

308. Target insignificant expenses first

Philip has a farm in a beautiful part of Western Australia where he grows avocados. One year his brother-in-law came down from the city during harvest time and volunteered to lend a hand. Phil told him to pick the lowest fruit first because they are the easiest to get to, anyone can do it (even the kids), you don't need any equipment such as stepladders and the fruit is often at its most plentiful.

Take a leaf out of the avocado farmer's book when looking at how to reduce your business overheads. Target less significant items such as office supplies, travel and entertainment expenses first. These are often the easiest to implement, every member of the team can be involved, few resources are required and the savings gained can be surprisingly large. Remember, it's the little things that can produce the biggest savings.

309. Every business needs a scrooge

Look at your finance department and you'll probably find someone whose sole purpose for existence is to make things as miserable as possible for anyone wanting to spend money. They have a passion and an undeniable skill for poring over miles of spreadsheets and picking out everything from the slightest discrepancy in expenditure through to major cost blow-outs. And to make matters worse, especially for salespeople, they have technology on their side giving them the ability to do and see more. Throughout my career I have watched many managers fall foul of company scrooges, but salespeople do need some controls. Many companies have found themselves in serious trouble because the sales staff have a 'make the sale at any cost' attitude, are concerned only with revenue and do not keep a close eye on expenses. Scrooges have a critical place in the larger scheme of any business. They can work hand in glove with the sales team and in doing so, they not only save money for your business but provide vital input into revenue-generating ideas. If your business doesn't have a scrooge, then go out and get one. Or, by adopting many of the ideas in this book, you can become your own version of the person whose job it is to keep everyone's eye on costs!

310. Ego has a price

How many small business owners have a big desk and a high-tech office chair, not to mention numerous other fancy bits and pieces of office furniture? Is it all really necessary? If you regularly have clients coming into your office, then maybe such extravagance can be justified, but question whether it really applies to your business. It is wise to control the ego—your status as a small business owner and entrepreneur is better reinforced by what you achieve than by having a flash office.

311. No frills cuts your bills

Your business doesn't have to have a Rolls Royce image to be successful. In fact, many businesses take the plain and simple approach and still produce a quality product, provide great service and achieve excellent profits.

Antonio owns a barbershop in the centre of the city. His shop is no bigger than a storeroom, all the mirrors are cracked, the chairs are old and worn, the walls could do with a fresh coat of paint and the magazines left lying around for his customers to read are tattered, torn and several years old. Faded pictures of James Dean and Elvis Presley (the kings of great hair) are taped to the wall and paint is peeling off the ceiling. Antonio himself is never seen wearing anything other than faded cargo pants and shirt, sleeves rolled to the elbows. Every day a long line of customers wait to pay $8 to have their locks trimmed by Antonio himself. Businessmen, school children, the elderly, teenagers and backpackers—Antonio caters to them all. His less than impressive surroundings have not detracted from the success of his business. On the contrary, his no frills approach, friendly service, cheap prices and great haircuts make for a winning combination. He also saves a great deal on running costs.

Remember, no frills cuts your bills. Or, as a friend of mine says about his no frills lawnmowing business—ugly is profitable!

312. Price increases cost you money

Be just as vigilant about keeping track of any price increases introduced by your suppliers as you are about looking for discounts and promotions. It is easy to get caught up in the daily challenges of running your business and not take the time to calculate the impact any price increase will have on your bottom line. Even small increases can have a significant effect, so the rule here is—take note of all increases and do the sums. Work out the exact dollar figure and then decide whether it is worth looking around for another supplier.

Paul runs a popular inner city restaurant and bar. One day he received a letter from a supplier informing him that the price of the consumable items (straws, toothpicks, paper napkins, etc.) that he purchased from them was about to increase. The increase at first glance seemed insignificant, so Paul just filed it in his 'Keep in view' file. On going through some paperwork later in the month he found the letter and, with a bit of time on his hands, set about calculating what the increase would mean to his business over the course of the coming year, using the past twelve months consumption of those items as a guide. He conservatively calculated the small price rise would cost his business an added $1200. Armed with this information, he sought out another supplier who was able to provide the products for much the same price as he used to pay.

Good planning and quick thinking can also save your business money when price increases are imminent.

Jan is the national marketing manager for a major consumer products manufacturer. Every two months the company mails out a newsletter to more than 20 000 customers. Jan was aware that Australia Post was about to increase the price of a standard postage stamp by 5c two weeks prior to the date when the next customer newsletter was due out. As the increase in postage represented an increase of $1000 to her postage bill, Jan moved the deadline for the newsletter ahead by three weeks and ensured it was posted out to customers at the old price.

313. A penny saved is a penny earned

This should become the war cry for all small business owners and managers. In fact, I prefer to rephrase it as 'a dollar saved is five bucks back in your pocket'. If your business has a 20 per cent profit margin, then a mere $1000 reduction in your costs is equivalent to $5000 in added revenue you would have to generate to get the same return. So how many pennies can you save?